THE DERVISHES OF TURKEY

THE DERVISHES
OF TURKEY

BY

LUCY M.J. GARNETT

with a Foreword by
OMAR M. BURKE

THE OCTAGON PRESS
LONDON

ISBN 0 863040 52 7

First Published in this Edition 1990

Printed and bound in Great Britain

Foreword

For a quarter of a century, The Octagon Press has specialised in books and monographs on the Sufis and Sufism.

These have enabled us to distinguish that there are three kinds of book in this field, often confused with one another:

A. Sufi books, intended to instruct, directly or indirectly and written by Sufis for that purpose;

B. Books written by outsiders, such as orientalists, which cannot instruct in the Sufi manner. The writers are never aware of the method of extracting currently relevant materials from traditional ones, 'the content from the container';

C. Documentation, constituting mainly former literary and other manifestations of Sufism, 'the museum materials'. Both in the East and West, imitators (and sincere copiers) have tried to base whole 'schools' and 'orders' on these superseded materials.

This present book has all the faults and all the virtues of categories B and C; and we should bear in mind that there are many people, in both East and West, who do not even suspect the existence of Category A materials.

The reason for this lack of information is mainly because all systems of religious and metaphysical organisation other than the Sufi one rely upon the mechanical reproduction of texts, mantrams, prayers, teachings and so on. None of the major schools traditional in the West has any conception of 'instrumental' materials. The conception that the teacher chooses what materials apply to his time and which to his particular student(s) is utterly foreign.

Anyone familiar with the field will know that, in East and West, dozens, perhaps hundreds, of books on Sufism exist, most of them completely out of tune with Sufism itself: yet all of them finding an echo in some circles, in certain psychologies. In short, these books – and many supposedly Sufi teachings – exist because there is a public for them, not because they have anything more than entertainment value.

This present book is fascinating on several counts, few of which were intended by the writer.

First of all, Ms Garnett clearly has almost no knowledge of any Eastern language, certainly not of Persian, Arabic or Turkish beyond the most element-ary. This is shown by the fact that (page 102) she imagines that Alif and Lam are the first and last letters of the alphabet in these languages. They are not. How much of a European language would you determine someone to know if he/she wrote 'A and P are the first and last letters of the Latin alphabet'?

Other grotesque mistakes abound; for instance when the well-known warcry 'Either a hero or a martyr!' is rendered as 'O Victors! O Martyrs!' This is due to an elementary confusion of the word 'Ya' (O) with the form 'Ya . . . Ya' ('either . . . or') in Persian.

Much of the information, collected in Ottoman Turkey in the early part of this century, is interesting where (though rarely) it is reliable. One of the most useful aspects of this book is to show just how near-illiterate Western writers and 'specialists' were. This helps to explain why for the West – and many Eastern imitators – Sufi affairs are so confusing and confused.

Eastern words are spelt sometimes in their French transliteration, sometimes in the Turkish style, sometimes (as in 'Khalif') in semi-English and semi-Arabic coinages.

Ms Garnett imagines that a Sufi thinks that he is God (p 6), which is little short of lunatic. In whole sections, there are errors on literally every page. She has the Caliphs Abu Bakr and Ali using Turkish words, which they would not have known.

The 'Uwaisi' are not an 'Order' at all (page 2). Sufism, as plentifully established, is not 'out of keeping with Islam'. And so it goes on.

A further advantage in this book as source material is the fact that many of the errors which appear in orientalist and other literary work during the 20th Century appear to have been copied from this book. And this in spite of the fact that it breaks almost every canon of scholarly instruction: 'check your sources'; 'verify your materials'; 'unify your terminology';'distinguish between opinion and fact' and so on.

Originally entitled 'Mysticism and Magic in Turkey', the present title is more relevant: Sufis are not mystics in the sense in which the word is used in English; still less are they magicians.

Omar Burke.

" O Allah ! Dervish let me live, and Dervish die,
and in the company of Dervishes raise Thou me to
Life Eternal ! "—*Prayer of* JAMI.

" Man, to express his most fervent adoration of
the Deity, uses the expressions with which he is wont
to address the object of his earthly affections ; he has
but the fire of earth to kindle in sacrifice to Heaven."—
The Dabistan I, clxii.

" They [the Sûfis] profess eager desire, but are
without carnal affections ; and they circulate the cup
which is no material goblet ; for with them all things
are spiritual, all is mystery within mystery."—
JELĀLŪ-'D-DĪN.

" The ONE remains, the many change and pass ;
   Heaven's light for ever shines, earth's shadows fly ;
   Life, like a dome of many coloured glass,
   Stains the white radiance of eternity."—SHELLEY

PREFACE

MY aim in this volume has been to give a thoroughly impartial account of the Dervishes of Turkey, so far as my knowledge of their principles and practices will allow, neither unduly concealing their lower, nor unduly exalting their higher aspects. And I would fain hope that this brief study of the Mystics of Islam may be found to have not only a speculative and religious, but also a practical and political interest. In controversies with respect to Islam and Civilisation, no account is usually taken of the Mystical side of this Creed as a native element of antagonism to the most essential doctrines of Islam. Widespread as is this unorthodox mysticism, it has been, and still is compelled to keep itself to a certain extent hidden. Events may, however, possibly, sooner or later, bring it to the surface, and endow it with practical significance. For as in the Christian West there has ever been a continuous protest both on the intellectual side by philosophers, and on the religious side by mystics, against the more distinctively Semitic doctrines of Christianity, so it has also been in the Moslem East in the Schools of the Dervishes, both among the Persians and the Ottomans. And as this speculative

protest by the Monks of Islam has not been without
practical results in Persia, so may it likewise be
expected to have corresponding results in Turkey.
From the Sūfism of the Dervish Orders sprang the
movement of Bābism, the initiation of which was
contemporary with the European revolutionary
uprising of '48. This movement, which was sup-
pressed with the most barbarous atrocities, gave
greater promise than any other event connected
with the East of that only possible kind of regeneration—regeneration from within. And should a
movement similar to that of Bābism, and, like it,
derived from the Sūfism of the Dervishes, break
out in Turkey, its importance will, it is to be hoped,
be better understood in Europe than was that of
Persian Bābism.

L. M. J. G.

CONTENTS

CHAPTER I

THE DERVISH ORDERS AND THEIR TENETS

> " Under an alien name
> I shadow One upon whose Head the crown
> Was, and yet Is, and Shall be ; whose Decree
> The Kingdoms Seven of this world, and the Seas,
> And the Seven Heavens alike are subject to.
> All joy to him who, under other name,
> Instructed us that Glory to disguise
> To which the initiate scarce dare lift his eyes ! "
>
> JĀMĪ, *Salaman and Absal.*

ALTHOUGH the second century of the Mohammedan era has been assigned by various students of the Sūfi Philosophy as the date of its origin, societies of mystics would appear to have existed in Islam from its very foundation. For it is recorded that, in the first year of that era, a number of the followers of the Prophet formed themselves into a Brotherhood for the ostensible practice of certain religious exercises of penitence and physical mortification. The word " Dervish " is, in Persian, synonymous with " beggar," and denotes also a person who voluntarily impoverishes himself for the benefit of others. The Khalifs Ali and Abu Bekr, actuated

1

2

by the desire to fulfil literally that precept of the
Koran which says that " He is the best of men who
is most useful to his fellow-men," gave up their
worldly goods to the common use, and entered upon
a career of service to others, calling themselves
Safa bashis[1] to indicate the purity of their lives.
The members of these Fraternities took, however,
a vow of fidelity to the Prophet and his doctrines,
and continued to perform their duties as citizens,
meeting occasionally for the performance of the
religious exercises peculiar to each congregation.
The leaders appointed their successors in office
under the title of *Khalifeh ;* and these in their turn
transmitted the rule of the Fraternity to the most
venerable, or the most spiritually gifted, among
its members.

Apart from the attraction of the Sūfi doctrines,
a life passed in retirement from the world for the
purpose of contemplation and devotion appears to
have always been congenial to the Oriental mind ;
and this natural tendency proved stronger than the
injunction of the Prophet prohibiting monasticism
among his followers.   For, even during Mohammed's
lifetime, many of the followers of Abu Bekr and Ali
abandoned the rules of the primitive fraternities
and formed monastic societies, the first Order of
Austere Anchorites being founded in the thirty-
seventh year of the Hegira (A.D. 659) by Sheikh
Uwais of Yemen, who gave out that the Angel

[1] Silvestre de Sacy, *Journal des Savants*, 1821, p. 724,
and D'Ohsson, *Tableau Général de la Turquie*.

Gabriel had commanded him, in a vision, to with-
draw from the world and consecrate himself to a
life of seclusion and penitence. The celestial
visitant at the same time communicated to this
ascetic the rules of the Order he was to found, which
included abstinence from food, and even the most
innocent pleasures, seclusion, and the recital of a
great number of prayers by day and night. To
these mortifications he voluntarily added the loss
of his teeth, requiring the same sacrifice from his
disciples, an ordeal which naturally prevented his
making proselytes of any but the most fanatical,
notwithstanding the Sheikh's high reputation for
learning and piety; and the sect never spread
beyond Yemen, where it originated. It, however,
greatly contributed to the institution of other
monastic orders by the more earnestly minded of
the followers of Abu Bekr and Ali.

The second century of the Hegira was the era of
a great religious movement. On one side was
developed a scepticism and unbelief that shook
Islam to its foundations, while, on the other hand,
mysticism acquired increasing power. This century
gave birth to a multitude of sects, and has accordingly been fixed upon, as before mentioned, as the
commencement of the system of religion and
philosophy professed by the Sūfis. Their recognised founder was Abu Saïd Abulkhair, who lived
at the end of that and the beginning of the next
century, and founded a monastic institution into
which he gathered those whose mode of thinking

resembled his own, and laid down rules for their guidance. There is, however, much disparity of opinion as to whether Sūfism, as it now exists, was, as asserted by the Sūfis themselves, instituted by him. In any case it is probable that the sect did not long remain within the limits of orthodox piety. This was, indeed, impossible. For the Sūfi philosophy, as must be admitted, was entirely out of keeping with the creed of Mohammed. And the mysticism of the early Moslems, so tender and full of sentiment, became gradually transformed into Pantheism, an equally natural consequence of its inherent tendencies and of the action upon Islam of older religious systems.

In the ninth century of our era, the partisans of this doctrine were divided into two branches, the chief of the one being Abū Yezid, or Bayazid Bestemi, who is revered as the *Pir*, or founder of the *Bestemi* Order, and of the other, Djouneïd. Bayazid Bestemi openly preached a Pantheism irreconcilable with revealed religion, and proclaimed more explicitly than any other Sūfi teacher had done the divine nature of man. Among the expressions he made use of are the following :—

" I am an ocean without bottom and without shore, without beginning and without end."

" When men imagine that they are adoring Allah, it is Allah who adores Himself."

" The seed of Sūfism was sown in the days of Adam ; it sprang up in those of Noah ; blossomed under Abraham ; and, at the time of Moses the grapes began to be formed. They came to maturity in the days of Jesus, and in those of Mohammed was the wine pressed from them. Those of the Sūfis who have loved this Wine have drunk of it until self-consciousness was drowned ; and they have then cried, ' Glory to me ! Is there anything greater than I ? ' or ' I am the truth, there is no God beside me ! ' "[1]

Djouneïd and his followers, on the other hand, while holding practically identical opinions, expressed themselves more prudently, and succeeded in uniting in an extraordinary manner the dogmas of the Koran with a system of philosophy which tended to destroy all religious practices, and reduce to nothing the merits of faith and works. To arrive at this result they had recourse to an expedient known as the *Ketman*, which has indeed rendered eminent service in all times and in all religions, but has been practised with greater success by the Sūfis than by any other sect. The terms of the dogmas of Islam were retained, but a totally different signification was given to them by the Sūfi teachers. Irreproachable Moslems in outward appearance, these mystics have ever excelled in the art of evading dangerous investigations, and, as M. Dozy remarks,[2] it " is rare that an adept, even when in

[1] Garcin de Tassy, *Mantic Uttair*, 4th ed., p. 5 ; and Sprenger, *Journal of the Asiatic Society of Bengal*, Vol. III, p. 134. Compare also the expressions of St. Augustine, of Duns Scotus Erigena, and of Eckhart, the Christian Mystic (1268-1327). See Vaughan, *Hours with the Mystics*.

[2] *Essai Sur l'Histoire de l'Islamisme*, p. 323.

an ecstatic state, compromises himself by proclaiming in public what is every Sūfi's private
belief—'*I am God.*'" By means of the *Ketman*
and allied methods of propaganda, Sūfism has
succeeded in permeating every class of Moslem
society, has had for centuries past its Chiefs, its
Councils, its Monks and its Missionaries, and presents
phases varied enough to suit every class of thought.

Hosain Ibn Mansur, also called Mansur Halladj,
who suffered martyrdom in 922, is revered by the
Sūfis as one of their greatest saints. He was a
disciple of Djouneïd, a Persian by birth, and grand-
son of a Zoroastrian or Magian. According to the
moderate Shias, his doctrine was that by practising
abstinence, avoiding all worldly pursuits and
pleasures, and mortifying the flesh, it is possible for
man to elevate himself through successive stages
until he becomes the equal of the Elect, and even
of the Angels. If he perseveres in this path until
nothing remains of his earthly nature, he receives
"the Spirit of God" as Jesus is held by Moslems
to have received it, and everything that he subsequently does is a divine action. The Shias also
maintain that he was put to death on account of
the extraordinary influence he exercised among the
upper classes, the Princes and their surroundings,
which aroused the jealous hostility of the orthodox
clergy. Halladj has not, indeed, been unfavourably
judged by the more liberal-minded among orthodox
writers. Gazzali, for instance, who, while he pro-
fessedly regarded the Sūfi philosophy with aversion,

expressed his preference for a religion which had its seat in the heart as compared with the dry orthodoxy expounded by the majority of the Ulema ; and he attributed even such assertions of Halladj as " I am the Truth, there is nothing in Paradise save Allah," etc., to his excessive adoration of the Deity. For the majority of orthodox writers of the period, however, this mystic was a blaspheming infidel and sorcerer. On his return to Bagdad after performing the customary pilgrimage to Mekka, strange stories of his miraculous powers were circulated in the city. He was credited with having raised the dead to life ; the *Djins*, it was said, were subject to him, and fulfilled his every command. Fearing his influence with the populace, and incited also, no doubt, by the legists, the Vizier Hamid induced the Khalif Moktadir to place Halladj and his followers at his disposal ; and notwithstanding the protection of the Lord Chamberlain, the mystic and his disciples were arrested.

When questioned, the disciples admitted that they looked upon their master as divine, seeing that he had raised the dead to life. But when Halladj himself was interrogated his reply was, " God forbid that I should lay claim to divinity or even to the dignity of Prophet. I am a man who adores the most high God."

The Vizier then summoned the Kadis and principal theologians, and demanded of them a sentence against Halladj. They replied that it was illegal to condemn the accused man without proofs of his alleged crime, as he had not confessed.

Foiled in his design, the Vizier had the mystic brought before him from time to time, and attempted in vain to draw from him some heretical admission. He found at length in his writings a statement to the effect that if a Moslem were prevented making the prescribed pilgrimage to Mekka, he might dispense with it by preparing a chamber in his own house in which to perform the rites connected with that duty ; these rites accomplished, he must further take to him thirty orphans, feed them on choice food, clothe them and bestow upon each one seven drachmas ; and the fulfilment of these duties would gain for him the merit of having performed the pilgrimage. On this being shown by the Vizier to the Kadi Abou Amr, he was scandalised, and asked, " Where hast thou found such an idea ? " Halladj mentioned a work by Hassan of Bassora. " It is a lie ! O infidel, whose blood it is lawful to spill," cried the Kadi. " The book thou namest was explained to us at Mekka by one of the Doctors ; but what thou hast written was not contained in it ! "

The Vizier seized eagerly upon the epithet " Infidel," used by the Kadi, and demanded a sentence of death from him. The Kadi at first demurred, saying that such was not his meaning ; but the Vizier insisted, and finally obtained a warrant for the execution of Halladj, signed by the Kadi and the other legists. In vain Halladj sought to prove his condemnation unjust. "You have not the right," he exclaimed, "to shed my blood. My faith is that of Islam; I believe in the *Hadis* (traditions) on which I have written works that may be found at all the booksellers. I have always acknowledged the Four Imāms, and the Four Khalifs. I call God to my aid, that my life may be spared!" His protests were unavailing. The Vizier hastened to bring the *fetvas* of the legists before the Khalif, who ordered that Halladj should die by scourging. He received a thousand strokes, after which his hands and feet were cut off, and subsequently his head, and his body committed to the flames. The disciples of Halladj, however, refused to believe that their revered master was dead. They maintained that a person resembling him had suffered in his place, and that he would show himself again after forty days. Some declared that they had seen him on the road to Nahrawan, mounted on an ass, and that he had said to them, "Be not like those foolish men who believe that I have been scourged and put to death."

Let us now turn to the Sūfi version of the story :—

"The name of Halladj was in everyone's mouth; they saw the miracles that he did, and an immense multitude followed him. And how should it have been otherwise? Returning from a pilgrimage, he happened to be crossing the desert with four hundred Sūfis. His companions said to him one day, 'We have nothing to eat, and we are hungry; we would like a roast lamb.'

" 'Sit down,' said the Saint.

" When they were seated, he placed his hand behind his back and gave to each one a roast lamb and two small hot loaves. They ate, and then asked for dates.

" ' Shake me,' said the Saint.

" They did so, and there fell from him fresh dates in such quantities that they sufficed for all the company.

" But there were those who were envious of the wonderful gifts of Halladj. These slandered him before the Khalif, and the Doctors of Bagdad condemned him to death because he had said 'I am the Truth.' They desired him to say 'It is He who is God,' and he replied, 'Yea, He is all things.'

" He was cast into prison. A multitude of people flocked to him for instruction, until, after the lapse of a year, it was forbidden to visit him. The first night of his imprisonment, he was not to be seen in his cell ; on the second, neither prisoner nor cell were to be seen. 'Where hast thou been ?' demanded the jailer of him. 'The first night,' he replied, 'I was with the Glorious Being, for that reason thou sawest me not ; on the second, the Glorious Being was with me, so thou sawest neither me nor the cell. To-day I am sent here to satisfy the law ; come and do to me what thou art commanded.' "

It is also related that when he arrived at the prison six hundred persons were confined there. " I will deliver you," he said. "Why deliverest thou not thyself?" they asked. "I am in the chains of God, and I have a companion, a faithful guardian. I have only to desire it, and at a sign my fetters will fall from me." He made a sign and the fetters of all the prisoners fell. "But the door is closed," they said. "How shall we depart?" Halladj having made another signal, the doors opened, everyone went out, and he was left alone. "Why departest thou not also?" he was asked. "I have a secret," he replied, "which I must impart only to him who is able to guard a secret."

On the following day the Khalif, learning what had happened, exclaimed, "He will do mischief; let him be hanged!"

They asked Halladj "Where are the prisoners?"

"I have set them free."

"Why hast thou too not departed?"

"Because Allah is offended with me."

The Khalif then gave the order to scourge him. He received six hundred strokes, and at each stroke a voice was heard crying, "Fear nothing, Halladj!" A hundred thousand persons had assembled on the road by which he was to pass to the scaffold. His eyes wandered over them, and he cried, "*God! God! God! I am God!*"

"What is true love?" a Dervish asked of him.

"That shalt thou learn to-day, to-morrow, and the day after," was the reply.

"Give me a remembrance of thee," begged a youth.

" The men of this world," replied the martyr,
" aspire after good works. Do thou aspire after a
thing of which an indivisible atom is worth more
than the collective good works of angels and men—
the knowledge of true science."

While speaking, Halladj danced and waved his
hands. " What manner of walking is this ? " he
was asked. " Am I not going to the place of my
sacrifice ? " was his reply, and he broke out into the
following mystical song :—

Say not, my Friend is heedless of my pain ;
The Cup He gives to me He too doth taste. [1]
Like host that with his guest the wine doth drain.
Yet, while the Cup goes round, the block and sword appear.
Such fate is his who with the Dragon [2] drinks,
While ardent shines the summer sun [above the plain].

When he placed his foot upon the first step of
the scaffold, Halladj exclaimed, " Behold man's
ladder to Heaven ! " He adjusted his girdle,
removed his *taiksan*—the drapery covering his head
and shoulders— turned his face towards Mekka, and
with uplifted hands uttered an inaudible prayer.
He then mounted the ladder. The people threw
stones at him, but he uttered no word of complaint
or reproach. When, however, the Sūfi Chibli, also
a disciple of Djouneïd, threw mud at him, he heaved
a sigh. " Thou dost not sigh when thou art struck
with stones, why sighest thou when they throw but

[1] Evidently signifying that God, being present in the
individual, sacrifices Himself.

[2] The Dragon, a sign of the Zodaic, here represents the
Deity.

mud at thee ? " he was asked. "They who take up stones," replied the martyr, "know not what they do, so that does not afflict me ; but Chibli knows that he sins, when he throws but mud." When his hand was cut off, he smiled and said, " It is not difficult to cut off the hand of him who is in chains ; it would require greater dexterity to deprive him of the qualities which raise him to the highest heaven." His feet were cut off. He still smiled, saying, " I have still two other feet to carry me to the Two Worlds, cut them off if you can !" When deprived of his hands, he rubbed his cheeks and arms with his bloody wrists ; and when questioned as to the meaning of this action, he replied, " I have already lost much blood, and my cheeks will soon become pale. I am unwilling you should imagine that they are blanched by terror, and I wish to leave you with rosy cheeks. Dark red is the colour of men." " But why," they persisted, " dost thou besmear thy arms with thy blood ? " " I do but perform the *abtest* [1]—the ablutions of love should be made with blood."

When he had been deprived of his eyes, and his executioners were preparing to cut out his tongue, he desired to speak once more ; and while the mob continued to assail him with stones, he cried, " Great God ! Reject them not because they afflict me thus. Praise to Thee, because, for my love of Thee, they have cut off my hands and my feet.

[1] The Moslem ablution which precedes the prayers repeated five times daily by all good Moslems.

When my head is severed from my body, grant that I may see Thy face." His last words were, " The only thing required by the Only One, is, that men declare Him to be the Only One."[1]

Such is the version given by the Sūfis of the martyrdom of Halladj. They look upon him as one of the most eminent representatives of their doctrines, having shown that death, and above all, the most cruel death, is the happiest thing that can befall a Sūfi ; for by it his soul is delivered from its prison, the body, and " the Lover " attains that " eternal union " with the " Beloved " which he has so long and so ardently desired.

Another legend says that an inspired Sūfi asked the Almighty why He permitted Mansūr Halladj to suffer. The reply was, "It is the punishment for the revealer of secrets." It is also related that when the Saint was about to be impaled in addition to his other tortures, the executioners could not perform their duty. In vain they endeavoured to seize him ; his body always eluded their grasp, and appeared seated in a composed posture in the air at some distance from the stake. While this was occurring on earth, his soul sought the regions of Paradise. He was accosted by the Prophet, who admitted that he had arrived at the highest stage, that of *Wisāl*, or " Union," and that his declaration that he was God was true. Mohammed, however, entreated him, for the sake of practical religion, which was necessary for unenlightened mortals, to

[1] Dozy, *Essai sur l'Histoire de l'Islamisme*, p. 234 *et seq.*

allow himself to be impaled. The soul of the holy
man accordingly, convinced by the words of the
Prophet, returned to earth to reanimate his body,
and suffer the death to which he had been sentenced
by his earthly judges. [1]

Similar conceptions of Oneness with the Deity
are expressed in a modern work by a Turkish
mystic, of which the following paragraph may serve
as an example :—

"And he [Jewād] laid his head on the pillow of
the quest of inspiration. Straightway he opened
his eyes, and found himself lying on a shore near a
vast city. He rose, and wondering, said to himself,
' My life !   Surely I was in my room . . . and this
city that is before me resembles not ours. *There is
no strength nor power save in Allah.* [2] Am I in a
vision ? '   In a single moment poor Jewād forgot
all that he had known—those spiritual sciences and
strange arts that he had learned and practised for
so long, all his wisdom and attainments, his manifest
gifts, his initiation into the Arcana ; nay, even what
he had learned and comprehended by means of his
five outer and inner senses ; and he stood as though
new born from his mother, gazing around him in
confusion." [Jewād then meets an aged man, who
conducts him into the city and shows him all its
beauties, and finally introduces him into the palace
of the King.] "The happy Jewād had left him no

[1] Malcolm, *History of Persia*, Vol. II, p. 281.
[2] A customary Moslem formula when surprised or
startled.

eye to see, or understanding to observe, or comprehension to know, or tongue to speak. When he entered the Royal Presence and raised his eyes to look upon the beauty of the King, he saw that he who sat upon the indescribable Throne was—HIMSELF."[1]

The twelfth century of the Christian era gave birth to two very important Orders—the Kādiri, and the Rūfā'i. The founder of the former, Abdul Kādr of Ghilan, besides being an eminent mystic, was a man of great learning, and numbered among his disciples his nephew Seyyïd Achmet Rūfa, who subsequently founded the· Rūfā'i—better known to Europeans as the " Howling Dervishes "—on whom he is said to have conferred the faculty of miraculously healing the wounds which the devotees of this Order inflict upon themselves during their extraordinary religious frenzies.

In the following century the gifted mystic poet Jelālū-'d-Dīn, surnamed " Er Rumi,"[2] established at Konieh, the capital of the Seljoukian Sultans, the Order of the *Mevlevi*—the so-called " Dancing Dervishes," in connection with the Royal College of which he was the Principal. After the incorporation of that city in the Ottoman Empire this Society became exceedingly flourishing. Endowed and honoured by the Ottoman as it had previously been by the Seljoukian Sultans, and constituting as it did the University of the Empire, state dignitaries

[1] *The Story of Jewād*, translated by E. W. Gibb.

[2] " The Roman," from his place of residence in *Rōm*, the Eastern Empire, which retained that name for centuries after the Turkish Conquest.

were proud to call themselves its graduates, and lay members of the *Mevlevi* Order of Dervishes. Even Grand Viziers did not disdain to don the *kulah* and vestments of the Brethren of Love, and take part in their mystical gyrations.

Although, as above remarked, the Sūfi principles enunciated by Bayazid Bestemi and Djouneïd are professed generally by the higher grades among the Dervishes, some of the Orders hold doctrines more purely mystical, and others more purely pantheistic than the rest. Of the more purely mystical, the Nakshibendi and Khalveti Orders are the chief representatives. Abu Bekr, the first Khalif, is looked upon as the *Pir*, or founder of the former Order, and Ali, the third Khalif, of the latter. The successful establishment of other communities having caused the extinction of the two original Fraternities, they had remained unrepresented, the former until the thirteenth, and the latter until the fourteenth century, when Mohammed of Nakshibend and Omer Khalvet respectively founded Orders which assumed their names. The rule observed by the Nakshibendi Dervishes is held to be in strict accordance with that instituted by Abu Bekr, and the members of this Order live in their own homes and pursue their ordinary avocations, meeting only at stated times for the performance of religious exercises. And though devotion does not in Turkey at the present day, as formerly, engage the attention of men of all ranks, this Order has remained one of the most numerous and popular in the Empire.

The Order of the Khalvetis, although professing to be a revival of the primitive congregation of the Khalif Ali, practise a much more rigid austerity than was compatible with the rule originally observed of remaining in the world and fulfilling the ordinary duties of citizens. Its members undertake to live much in retirement, and to devote a great part of their time to solitary contemplation. A legend of this Order relates that, as its *Pir* was on one occasion leaving his cell after a prolonged period of mystical meditation, he heard a celestial voice behind him saying, " O Omer Khalvet ! Why dost thou leave us ? " and, accepting this as a divine injunction, he resolved to consecrate the rest of his days to such contemplation, and to institute an Order bearing his name, which signifies " Retirement."[1]

The Order of the Bektāshis which, in addition to its numerous adherents among the Osmanlis, is said to include in its ranks some 80,000 Albanian Moslems, was instituted about the same period by Hadji Bektāsh—" Bektāsh the Pilgrim "—one of the many learned men whom the munificence of the early Ottoman Princes attracted to Asia Minor from Khorassan. Orchan, who is said to have attributed many of his victories to the presence in his army of this holy man, built for him at Sivas a monastery and college, and sought his approval and blessing on every undertaking. And when the Emir[2] had

[1] J. B. Brown, *The Dervishes*.
[2] The title of " Sultan " was not assumed by the earlier Ottoman rulers, who styled themselves simply " Princes."

enrolled that first fair young band of Christian boys which was destined to develop into " the strongest and fiercest instrument of imperial ambition ever devised upon earth," [1] he led them to the abode of the saintly Sheikh, and begged of him to bestow upon them his blessing. With his arm, draped in the wide sleeve of his mantle, stretched over the head of a youth in the front rank, Hadji Bektāsh thus addressed the Emir :—

" The troop which thou hast now formed shall be called *Yeni Sheri* (' New Troop '). Their faces shall be white and shining, their right arms strong, their sabres keen, and their arrows sharp. They shall be fortunate in battle, and never leave the field save as victors." [2]

The *Yeni Sheri*, or Janisseries, in consequence of this benediction, remained, until the destruction of their corps in 1826, closely incorporated with the Order founded by this famous Sheikh. [3]

The various Dervish Orders were not, it would seem, originally designated, as now, by the names of their respective founders, but by the principles they severally professed; but as each community grew in course of time more distinct from the rest, the name of the *Pir* was adopted to distinguish its members. The twelve communities which existed at the time of the foundation of the Ottoman Empire

---

[1] Creasy, *History of the Ottoman Turks*, pp. 14-15.
[2] Von Hammer, *Histoire de l'Empire Ottomane*, Vol. II, p. 71.
[3] See below, p. 187.

have now increased to thirty-six, with as many subordinate branches.

The *Kalenderi* Dervishes, or " Kalenders," as they are often called by translators, are not, strictly speaking, an Order, as they are not descended from either of the original congregations. Their founder, Kalender Yussūf-Andalusi, was a native of Andalusia, and for long a disciple of Sheikh Hadji Bektāsh, from whose brotherhood he was finally expelled on account of his overbearing temper, and arrogant behaviour. He then made unsuccessful attempts to gain admittance to the *Mevlevi* Order, and ended by establishing on his own authority a Brotherhood the rules of which included the obligation of perpetual wandering, and of entertaining an eternal hatred against the Orders from which he had been excluded. The title of *Kalender*, which he assumed and bestowed on his followers, signifies " pure," implying the purity of heart, spirituality of soul, and exemption from worldly contamination which Yussūf required in his disciples—qualities somewhat at variance, one might suppose, with the above-mentioned obligation. This same title of *Kalender*, it may be remarked, is also given to Dervishes of all Orders who are distinguished among their brethren for superior spirituality. It is this class of " enlightened " beings which has produced so many dangerous fanatics in every age of Mohammedanism. From it have come the assassins of Sultans, Viziers, and Grandees of the Empire, and all the unconscious imposters who, under the title of *Mahdi*, have misled thousands and desolated whole countries by their supposed prophecies and divine revelations.

The attainment of a high degree of sanctity being thus the aim of every true Dervish, he seeks, in order to attain this, to lead a life of sinless retirement from the world, and spends his days and nights in prayer and meditation. Fully impressed with the possibility of ultimately attaining intimate divine communion, the aspirant after it looks upon every mundane interest as unworthy of consideration ; his mind becomes more and more completely absorbed in mystic contemplation ; and as the result of his constant invocation of the name of the Deity, he hears, even when in the midst of a noisy crowd, no other sound but *Allah ! Allah !* unless, indeed, it be some divine command addressed to him in return. The more destitute a Dervish is of worldly goods, the fewer are his ties to earth ; the more emaciated his body with privation and fasting, the greater his advance in spirituality ; the ills of existence affect him not, and death has for him no terrors. His solitude is cheered by the presence of angelic visitors who impart to him wondrous things hidden from the ken of ordinary mortals. Or they are the bearers of direct messages from the Deity, who thus makes known to his servants His holy Will concerning men ; and when commanded to do so, the Dervish fearlessly denounces, in the name of Allah, the great ones of the earth who, by their misdeeds, have incurred the divine displeasure.

CHAPTER II

THE SPIRITUAL HIERARCHY

"A Saint is aware of every thought of the King's heart, and of every secret on earth or in heaven."—*Saying of* JELĀLŪ-'D-DĪN.

IT is noteworthy that Mohammed, in proclaiming himself to be the Messenger of Allah, connected himself with the past as the Last of the Prophets. The Moslem hierarchy of inspired Seers begins with Adam, and includes the patriarchs Noah and Abraham as well as the greater Jewish Prophets and Christ, each successive one being esteemed greater than his predecessor. But in addition to this historical hierarchy of Prophets there exists, in Moslem belief, another of an entirely mythical character—a succession of saintly beings unto whom the Will of Allah has been revealed, and through whose instrumentality the destinies of mankind are governed. Supreme among these Saints of the Moslem Calendar is Khizr, or Khidhr-Elias, a mythical personage who from time immemorial has in various forms and under different names, filled a prominent place in the religions of the world. This protean Saint, or Demi-god, appears to be identifiable with the Prophet Elijah, or Elias, as well as with the Christian St. George, who, in his turn, has been identified with Horus.[1] Khidhr is held to have

[1] Comp. Lenormant, *Origines* ii, p. 12 ; Clermont-Ganneau, *Rev. Arch.* xxx, pp. 388-397 ; Guyard, *Rev. de l'Histoire des Religions*, 1880, p. 344 ; Gaston Paris, *Acad. des Inscriptions*, etc., 1880, pp. 91-116.

had his original abode in the terrestrial Paradise which contained a tree of Life and a Fountain of Life ; and having eaten of the fruit of the one and drunk of the water of the other he became immortal.[1] As the wisest of created beings, he was consulted by Moses, who, accompanied by Joshua, journeyed to a place where two rivers met, or, according to other writers, to an " Isle of the Isles of the sea," where they found the Sage from whom Moses received the secret of the " True Path."[2] Another legend gives the following account of this journey :—

" The prophet of Israel, in one of his interviews with Allah on Mount Sinai, prayed for wisdom to comprehend the hidden mysteries. ' That is too hard a matter for thee,' replied the Almighty. But on the Prophet's insisting, He relented and said, ' Make then for thyself iron shoes and get ready a cooked fish. Then set out. Thou wilt walk until the shoes are worn out and the fish has returned to life, and then wilt thou find the man who shall instruct thee in the knowledge of mysteries.'

" Moses did as the Lord bade him, and, accompanied by St. John the Baptist, he set out. In the evening Moses and John ate some of the fish, yet the next day they found it again whole. After a long

[1] This " Water," " Fountain," " Stream," or " River of Life," said to exist in a Land of Darkness in the extreme East, is an Oriental myth alluded to in *Revelations* xxii. 1, and often made use of by Ottoman and Persian poets. It frequently occurs also in the folk-tales of South-Eastern Europe.
[2] See p. 104.

journey they arrived at a spot where two seas met.
Moses lay down to sleep, and John was watching
over him, when suddenly a drop of spray fell on the
fish, which immediately came to life again and
plunged into the sea. When Moses awoke he set
out again with John, who had told him nothing of
the resuscitated fish. Towards evening they stopped
to eat, but the fish was not there. St. John then
revealed what he had seen, and Moses returned to
the place where the fish had leapt into the sea.
There they found a man lying on the ground. Moses
saluted him respectfully, and the prostrate man
returned his salute, saying, ' Health to thee, Moses,
my father.'

" ' Who told thee that I am Moses ? '

" ' Allah, who has sent me to thee.'

" This man was Khidhr. ' What wilt thou with
me ? ' he asked.

" ' I will that thou instruct me in the knowledge
of mysteries. I will follow thee wherever thou
goest.'

" ' Thou canst not follow me,' said Khidhr, ' nor
art thou able to acquire the knowledge of mysteries.'

" ' I will follow thee, and I will strive to learn of
thee.'

" ' Thou mayest follow me on one condition only
—that thou meddle not in my business.'

" Moses accepted the condition. Then, sending
back John the Baptist to his own country, Moses
and Khidhr asked for passage on board a ship which
was about to set sail. The two men had no money,

and their clothes were ragged. The captain at first refused to take them on board, but finally yielded to their solicitations, and allowed them to sail with him.

" After a long voyage they arrived in a port ; but before going ashore Khidhr made a great hole in the vessel in which he had had a free passage.

" ' What injustice ! what wickedness ! ' thought Moses to himself.

" Khidhr, who reads the hearts of men, remarked to him, ' Said I not to thee that the knowledge of mysteries is difficult to acquire, and hast thou not promised to meddle not in my affairs ? '

" Moses held his peace.

" As they passed through a town, Khidhr perceived in a lonely spot a beautiful child asleep, and cut off its head. The soul of Moses revolted against this crime, but he said nothing. They left the town, and came to the country. Seeing a wall about to fall in ruins, Khidhr straightened it, and, with the help of Moses, left it in good repair.

" ' What folly,' thought Moses to himself, ' Khidhr kills an innocent child, and then repairs an old ruined wall in the fields ! '

" Khidhr was aware of the reflections of Moses. ' You find unjust,' he said, ' the deeds I have done in your company ; you are blaming me. I will explain to thee the motives of my conduct : Listen ! I scuttled the vessel in which we had a free passage. It belongs to five persons of whom three are orphans under age whose sole livelihood is the profit they derive from it. In the city where we landed is a tyrant who seizes upon every sound vessel which enters the port. The vessel which brought us, being unsound, he has let go on her way.

" ' I cut off the head of the sleeping child because, had he grown up, he would have been the cause of great misfortunes to his country and to its religion.

" ' We mended the ruined wall, and that seemed to thee labour thrown away. This wall belongs to some young children, and conceals a hidden treasure. Had it fallen down, the first passer-by would have found this treasure ; it will now stand firm till the children are grown up, and they will enjoy their own.

" ' I told thee that thou wert not able to follow me, or to acquire the knowledge of mysteries. Said I not truly ? Go thou on thy way.'

" And Khidhr disappeared."

Khidhr is also credited in Moslem belief with having led the Israelites out of Egypt and guided them through the Red Sea and the Desert, taking the place of the " pillars of cloud and of fire " in the Biblical account of this incident. Moslems also hold that Khidhr-Elias, as he is often termed, though really one single individual, has a dual personality. He is regarded as the special protector of travellers, being invoked under the former name by those journeying on the sea, and under the latter by those journeying on land. Both parts of this dual person-age are believed to be perpetually wandering over the world, Khidhr on the sea, and Elias on the

land, and to meet once a yea: at Mina, near Mekka,
on the day of the " Statior, of the Pilgrims." He
is thus connected with St Nicholas, who performs
the same good offices for the Greeks, and is the
special patron of sailors.[1] St. Nicholas is also
further confounded with "Ηλιos, with Ali, the nephew
of the Prophet, and with Phineas, the immortal
hero of Talmudic legend who is credited with the performance of twelve miracles, and, according to that
authority, destined, like Elias, to play an important
part at the end of the world. This belief would
appear to be illustrated in the question addressed
to Jesus by his disciples : " Why say the Scribes
that Elias must first come ? " and in His answer
that " Elias is come already and they knew him
not,"[2] as also in the popular Eastern belief in the
periodic incarnation of this mythical being.

Numerous instances are recorded in Moslem
literature and legend of the sudden appearances and
disappearances of Khidhr-Elias. By many he is
held to be always visibly present somewhere on the
earth, and like his prototype the Tishbite, is often
" carried by the Spirit of the Lord " from place to
place. Could he be recognised, a knowledge of the
secret of immortality might be demanded of him ;
but it is only a saintly man who can distinguish
Khidhr from another. A Moslem desirous of an

[1] A Greek couplet says of this Saint :—

> He to our aid comes on the sea,
> And on the land works wondrously.

[2] *Matt.* xvii. 10, 12.

interview with this mysterious being, must, according to Turkish popular belief, perform his devotions
during forty consecutive days under the central
dome of the mosque of St. Sofia at Constantinople,
and on the fortieth day he is certain to be rewarded
with a sight of Khidhr-Elias. Evliya Effendi,
" The Traveller," himself a member of a distinguished Dervish family, declares in his *Narrative* [1]
that " thousands of holy men have here enjoyed
the happiness of converse with that great Prophet."
And many are the quaint and fantastic legends
current in the Turkish capital concerning interviews
with this " Master of Secrets." [2]

One of these legends relates that a pious Turk
who had undertaken the quest of Khidhr, met, on
the fortieth day, in the vicinity of the mosque, a
stranger, who said to him, " The mosque is not yet
open ; Why comest thou to disturb the sleep of its
guardians ? "

" I come to seek Khidhr," he replied.

" Dost thou know him ? "

" I know him not."

" Then follow me, and I will show him to thee."

Khidhr—for it was indeed he whom the True
Believer had met—went on before him, and the
pious man observed that his feet left an imprint on
the stones over which he walked.

[1] *Narrative of Travels*, p. 60.
[2] One of these, more marvellous even than the following,
is given by Evliya Effendi, who concludes it with the
remark—" The proof rests with the relater." Part I,
pp. 60-63.

" Dost thou know what Khidhr can do ? " asked the stranger.

" No," replied the pious man.

" Khidhr can thrust his finger into stone even as I do."

His finger entered the stone as he spoke, and the stone " perspired " abundantly.[1]

" When thou seest a man who does wonders such as these, say to thyself, ' This is Khidhr ! ' and hold him fast."

" I will not fail," he replied, and his companion disappeared.

The pious man entered the mosque and related his adventure to its guardians.

" 'Twas Khidhr himself ! " they cried. " If thou see him again, fail not to hold him fast, and let him go only when he has fulfilled thy desire."

The man performed his devotions in the mosque for another forty days, and on the morning of the fortieth he met a stranger who accosted him as the other had done.

" I would see Khidhr," he again replied.

" What seekest thou from him ? " asked the stranger.

Then the pious man concluded that this was indeed Khidhr, and he seized and held him fast.

" I am not Khidhr," said the stranger.

[1] Stones into which Khidhr is believed to have thrust his finger are held to cure those afflicted with profuse perspiration. The sufferer inserts his finger into the cavity, strokes with it his forehead and eyelids, and, it is confidently asserted, " goes away cured."

" Yea, thou art he ! "

" I am not. Suffer me to go on my way, and I will show thee Khidhr."

" Yea, thou art indeed Khidhr," insisted the pious man. " Fulfil my desire, or I will proclaim aloud who thou art and others will then likewise seize and hold thee."

" I tell thee again I am not he whom thou seekest. Thou wilt see Khidhr on Friday in the mosque at the hour of the noontide *namaz*. He who shall place himself on thy right hand at the moment the public prayers begin will be Khidhr ; hold him fast." So saying, the stranger disappeared.

Friday came, and the True Believer repaired to the mosque of St. Sofia for the noontide prayer. Just as the service was beginning, a man, dressed as an Usher of the Sublime Porte, placed himself on his right. As they came out of the mosque the pious man seized the Usher, saying,

" Thou art Khidhr ! I will not let thee go ! "

The Usher stoutly denied that he was other than his dress betokened him, and did his best to get away from the pious man. A long struggle ensued. The two men wrestled, fell, and rose again, until they came to the cemetery outside the Adrianople gate of the city. The window of a *turbe* [1] stood open, and the usher climbed through it, closely followed by the pious man, who still held on to his clothing, and after various turns, they came into a splendid

[1] The mausoleum erected over the tomb of a reputed saint. Many famous Dervishes are buried in this cemetery.

subterranean hall. Round it were ranged forty sheepskin mats, thirty-eight of which were occupied by venerable-looking men. The stranger was the chief of the Forty, one of whom had just died, and the pious man was allowed to take his place.

" Thou mayst seat thee on any mat thou wilt save that which is reserved to me, said the Usher, who was the Sheikh of the Forty, as he and his companions prepared to go out on the morrow.

The pious man obeyed, and remained in the underground dwelling for eight days, during which he was left alone from morning until sunset. But on the eighth day the True Believer, moved by curiosity, seated himself on the sheepskin of the Chief. Suddenly he saw as in one glance the whole world with everything in and upon it, even to the innermost thoughts of men, and was filled with wonder and delight. As the hour for the return of the thirty-nine approached, he took another seat, where they found him.

" What hast thou done ? " they demanded in voices of thunder.

" I have done naught."

" Yea, thou didst sit in the forbidden seat."

" Nay, I did not," mendaciously replied the pious man.

But scarcely had he said the words than the hall became dark, and he found himself again in the cemetery outside the Adrianople gate.

An anecdote recorded by Eflaki [1] as a proof of the

[1] *Acts of the Adepts*, Redhouse's *Mesnevi*, p. 78.

exceptional spiritual gifts of Jelālū-'d-Dīn also illustrates the same belief regarding Khidhr. When this great Dervish poet was still quite young, he was one day preaching on the subject of Moses and Elias.[1] During the discourse one of his disciples noticed a stranger seated in a corner paying great attention, and every now and then exclaiming, " Good ! " " Quite true ! " " Quite correct ! " " He might have been the Third with Us Two ! " etc. It occurred to the disciple that this might be Khidhr-Elias. He therefore grasped his garment, and begged for his spiritual aid.

" Oh ! " said the stranger, " seek aid rather from your master, as we all do. Every mystic saint of Allah is the loving and admiring friend of Jelāl."

So saying, he disengaged his robe from the disciple's grasp, and instantly vanished.

The *Murīd* then went to pay his respects to his master, who at once addressed him with the words, " Elias and Moses and the Prophets are all friends of mine." The Dervish understood the allusion, and became thereafter a still more ardent follower of his Sheikh.

According to the mystical canon, there are always on earth a certain number of holy men who are admitted to intimate communion with the Deity. The one who occupies the highest position among his contemporaries is called the " Axis " (*Qūtb*) or " Pole " of his time. As Elias was in his day an " Axis," and indeed as such held a higher spiritual

[1] *Koran*, Chap. xviii. 59-81.

rank than all other *Qūtbs*, it is his privilege to appoint his successors in office.   This prevalent belief accords curiously with the biblical story of his investiture of Elisha with his own miraculous powers and offices, and of the subjection of all contemporary Prophets to both in turn, and forms a strong link in the chain with which the Dervishes connect their doctrines and powers with those of the Prophets, Seers, and Patriarchs of old.   These "Poles" are quite unrecognisable as such, save by other holy men, and may belong to any rank in life, as is illustrated in the following story told by Evliya Effendi.

When the terrible conqueror, Timour the Tartar, was marching against Broussa, the alarmed inhabitants asked the eminent Dervish, Emir Sultan,[1] who resided there, what would be the fate of their city.   The Sheikh replied that, as Broussa was under the special protection of Khidhr and of Eskedji Hodja,[2] these holy men must be informed of the approach of the enemy.   He accordingly sent a letter by the hand of one of his Dervishes to Eskedji Hodja, who was found in the Tartar camp. When the Saint, who was busy mending a torn garment, had read the missive, he stuck his needle into his turban, exclaiming, "Emir Sultan shall be obeyed!" and before he had finished putting his work into his bag, the camp was, at his unuttered

[1] Complimentary titles of "Pasha," "Emir," or "Sultan" were frequently bestowed on learned men in the palmy days of the Ottoman Empire. See pp. 61 and 167.
[2] Literally "The Patching-tailor Parson."

command, broken up. "For," adds the narrator, "this old tailor was a *Qūtb*, a ' Pole of Poles,' and a Chief among Saints."

Subordinate to the *Qūtb* are two holy beings who bear the title of "The Faithful Ones," and are assigned places on his right and left respectively. Below these is a quartette of "Intermediate Ones" (*Evtād*) ; and on successively lower planes are five "Lights" (*Envār*), and seven "Very Good" (*Akhyār*). The next rank is filled by forty "Absent Ones" (*Rijal-i-ghaib*), also termed "Martyrs" (*Shuheda*). When an "Axis" quits this earthly existence, he is succeeded by the "Faithful One" who has occupied the place at his right hand, and the vacancies thus caused are filled up from the successive ranks.

"The Absent Ones" are said to have a circular plan, or map, of the world, having for its centre the holy city of Mekka. It is divided into thirty sections corresponding with the days of the Mohammedan month, and on it are also denoted the points of the compass. The Forty set out from Mekka every morning in the direction indicated by their map for that day, returning before the end of twenty-four hours to make their report to the "Axis." Any one possessing a copy of their map can, by consulting it, ascertain where the "Absent Ones" may be found at a given time, and by placing himself in their path may obtain from them whatever spiritual boon he may desire. For to these holy men, who also bear the collective titles of "Lords of Souls," and " Directors,[1] is committed a spiritual supremacy over mankind far exceeding the temporal authority of earthly rulers. The transactions and designs of every individual are believed to be under their control, and must receive their approval, or at least permission, before they can be carried into effect. For they are the Deputies of the Prophets and Saints who have left the world, and to them is divulged the will of Allah with regard to the actions of men.

According to Mr. Lane's [2] account of these mystical beings the "Axis" is, like Khidhr, " often seen, but not recognised as such ; and the same is said of all who hold authority under him. He always has a humble demeanour and mean dress, and mildly reproves those whom he finds acting impiously, particularly those who have a false reputation for sanctity. Though he is unknown to the world, his favourite stations are well known, yet at these places he is seldom visible. It is asserted that he is almost constantly seated on the roof of the Ka'abah ; and though never seen there, is always heard at midnight to cry twice, ' O Thou most merciful of those

[1] Sadi thus refers in his *Gulistan* to these mystical beings. (I quote from Mr. Davis's translation.)

A group of Directors, in lonely retreat,
With their breath full of fire, although earthly their feet—
They root up a hill from its site, with a cry ;
And a kingdom demolish at once, with a sigh.
Like the wind they're unseen, and of hurricane speed ;
Like stones they are silent, and rosaries read.

[2] *The Modern Egyptians.*

who show mercy ! ' which cry is then repeated by
the *Moeddins* from the minarets of the temple ; but
a respectable pilgrim, whom I have just questioned
upon this matter, has confessed to me that he
himself has witnessed that this cry is made by a
regular minister of the mosque, yet that few pilgrims
know this : he believes, however, that the roof of
the Ka'abah is the chief station of the 'Axis.'
Another favourite resort of this revered and
unknown person is the gate of Cairo. Though he has
a number of favourite stations, he does not abide
solely at these, but, like Khidhr, wanders through
the world, among persons of every religion, whose
appearance, dress, and language he assumes ; and
distributes to mankind, chiefly through the agency
of the subordinate *Welees*, the evils and blessings
apportioned to each by his *Kismet*."

Mr. J. P. Brown also describes an encounter
which a Dervish friend of his had with one of
these " Lords of Souls," or, as he terms them,
" Spiritual Owners," while on a pilgrimage to the
tomb of the Khalif Ali. His name was Jemel-ed-
Dīn of Kūfa, and the Dervish described him as a
person of middle stature, perfectly naked, with
scanty hair and beard, of feeble frame, and
apparently some forty to fifty years of age. When
the Dervish came up with him in the desert and
alighted from his horse for the purpose of offering
his homage, the saint turned round suddenly, and
cried in a loud voice, " Go to Allah ! " The pilgrim
was too startled and frightened to kiss the hand of

the holy man as he had intended, and returned to Kūfa, which place he had passed on his way. On enquiring at the mosque there for the abode of this Saint, he was shown a spot near the tomb of the Khalif Ali's nephew, where he was said to sleep on a mat of date-palm leaves, with a stem for his pillow. The Dervish asked how he was supported, and in what way he passed his time ; but could obtain no further information about him, save that he came there every night to sleep, and left again in the morning for the desert. This person, it appears, died in 1882 (A.H. 1260,) and has been succeeded in his saintly rank by an individual of the name of Beder ed Dīn, who will live till 1902 (A.H. 1280) when the " Last of the Saints " will take his place. [1]

Below the " Absent Ones " is another class of saints called *Abdāls*, from among whom the higher ranks are recruited as vacancies occur. These persons would, I fear, in more highly civilised countries be termed idiots or lunatics. Orientals, however, treat with reverence what they cannot explain ; and, according to the popular belief, the *Abdāls* are beings so holy that their souls have already found their way to heaven, and their bodies are consequently left on earth without the guidance of ordinary reason. As none but Allah knows who has in reality been promoted to fill the place of a defunct " Absent One," any *Abdāl* may be credited with that honour. The result of this reputation

[1] *The Dervishes.*

for sanctity enjoyed by *Abdāls* is that they are allowed to wander at large over the country, sometimes half clad, sometimes completely naked, following the bent of their errant fancies ; and the wilder and more extraordinary their vagaries, the greater is their renown for virtue and holiness. They are no respecters of persons, but denounce with impunity high and low, pasha or peasant, who may chance to incur their anger or dislike ; and though the more enlightened portion of the public may estimate these maniacs at their just value, they will at the same time avoid any collision with them, as their abusive threats when excited are attributed by the ignorant to divine inspiration.

Many of those, however, who are termed *Abdāls*, or *Perishāns*, are in full enjoyment of all their faculties, but, possessed by an aversion for their fellow-men, shun their abodes, and, like the hermits of Christendom, retire to mountains and deserts where, fed perhaps on " locusts and wild honey " —though the popular belief credits them with the faculty of being able to dispense altogether with food—they live in harmony with wild animals whose fierceness or timidity they overcome by means of their wonderful spiritual powers.

A succession of famous *Abdāls* has existed in Turkey extending from the time of the conquest to the present day, and the renown of many has been so great that we find their sayings and doings chronicled by the historians and writers of their

times.   During the reign of Sultan Orchan, the most
famous were *Abdāl* Mousa and *Abdāl* Murad, who
were with the army at the conquest of Broussa,
and whose tombs in that city are still visited by
devout pilgrims.   The " Sultan of all Saint-fools,"
commonly called Sabah-Sabah, was, according to
Evliya Effendi, [1] the son of a sergeant of the Jani-
series, and lived in the reign of Mohammed IV.
Having foretold his father's death on the day before
it took place, the word *Sabah* (to-morrow) was
retained by him as his nickname.   During the Grand
Vizierate of Karā Mustapha, he one day made a
great disturbance at the *Divan* by clamouring for
the liberation of his mother, who had been imprisoned for smoking tobacco, a practice, it would
appear, not then permitted to women.   " Release,"
he cried, " the women, and imprison the men if
you will, for I have no father."   " Thus," adds the
narrator, " he got his mother released."

Among the many Saints and other Dervishes who
accompanied the army of Mohammed III in his
campaign into Hungary, was an individual who
held a Colonel's commission.   When the war was
over he was speechless for seven years, and then
was only heard to repeat the words *Yetmish grūsh*
(seventy piastres), by which name he was thereafter
called.   He, however, subsequently prophesied to
Sultan Murad IV that he would take Erivan and
lose it again within seven days.   This Sultan was
known to assert that, though " Yetmish grūsh "

[1] *Narrative of Travel.*

had remained behind in Constantinople, he perpetually heard in the camp the prophetic words of the *Abdāl*. This saintly personage affected the dress of a soldier of the Bosnian frontier, and possessed the strange faculty of walking about the muddy streets of the capital without soiling even the soles of his *babouches*—a miraculous feat, indeed, if the state of the streets in wet weather was then anything like what it is at the present day.

Another famous *Abdāl* of those times, Durmich Dédéh, frequented the Castle of Rumili, at the entrance of the Bosphorus, and sailors were in the habit of propitiating him on their arrival in port with an *oka* (about 2¾ lbs.) of meat. He advised ship captains concerning the voyages they were about to make. If they followed his counsel, it turned to their advantage ; but if they disregarded it, ill luck was sure to accompany them. Those who passed him on their way to the *Divān* were also forewarned, by his behaviour towards them, whether they were or were not likely to prosper that day in their suits at law. [1]

That this canonisation of persons of weak intellect still continues, will be seen from the following story, as related to Lady Blunt and myself by Sheikh Ali, a Bektāshi of Salonica. I give, as nearly as possible, a literal translation of his own words :—

" My younger brother had been, from his childhood, of an erratic and unmanageable disposition. It was impossible to teach him anything, and he

[1] *Narrative of Travel.*

spent the greater part of his time in roaming from village to village, fed by the charitable, but housed I know not how, and occasionally returning home to me for a few days. As he grew older, he became confirmed in these wandering habits, and was seldom at home. He returned one day from a prolonged excursion complaining that he felt unwell, and asked to be allowed to lie down in my room. He was very thirsty and feverish, and ere long smallpox declared itself. The elders of the *Tekkeh*, at my request, came in and prayed over him. When they had finished, he smiled, thanked them, and requested that they would come again in four days' time, at the same hour, for on that day, at noon, he would die. The Dervishes, deeply affected, promised to do as he wished, and withdrew. For the next three days he was unconscious, his sight failed, and I saw that his case was hopeless. On the fourth day, at the hour he had mentioned, he came to himself, and asked me to send for the Brethren. I did so, and they again prayed over him. Then, turning to me, he said, ' My brother, I have been a sore burden to you all my life. I pray you, make me *helāl*[1] (free gift) of all the bread I have eaten at your hands, so that I may depart in peace.' I made the *helāl*, holding the poor saint's head on my knees. He then said, ' I am content,' and breathed his last

[1] One of the ceremonies at a Moslem funeral is the giving of *helāl* by the friends and relatives of the defunct. It conveys pardon for any offence committed towards them, and is the Moslem equivalent for the Christian *requiescat in pace*.

just as the clock struck the hour of noon. My community pronounced him an *evliya*[1] (saint) and he was buried with the honour due to one who had held communion with Allah."

Patron saints also hold no unimportant place in this mystical hierarchy. They include, besides defunct Dervishes of peculiar holiness, all the more famous biblical characters ; and their protection is perhaps specially claimed by the numerous *esnafs* or trade guilds. Thus the Bakers, who, according to Evliya Effendi, have precedence over all other guilds of handicraftsmen, and enjoy the honourable title of " Columns of Faith," have for their patron Adam, who, say the Moslems, was forbidden to eat of the corn-tree in Paradise, but having transgressed the divine command, he was exiled to earth, where Gabriel brought again to him the corn, which he boiled and converted into soup. Hence the form of invitation usual now in the East : " Come, let us eat the Father's soup (*ash baba*) together ! " Gabriel then taught Adam to grind the corn and make it into bread.

The mythical Jemshid,[2] who is reputed to have lived a thousand years and to have invented three hundred arts, protects, among others, the Firework-makers. The patron saint of the Coffee-makers is

[1] This plural form of the Arabic word is popularly used as a singular noun.

[2] Jemshid was the fourth king of the first Persian dynasty mentioned in the *Shah Nameh*, where he is described as having been eminent in learning and wisdom. When he

Ebul Hassan Schaseli, who discovered the virtues
of the Mocha berry ; that of the Gardeners is Babá
Reten, a recluse of Mount Olympus, learned in
botany ; and that of the Dentists, or rather barber
tooth-drawers, Sheikh Uwais, mentioned in the
preceding chapter.

---

had reached the summit of his power and glory, he was
able to compel the very demons to labour for him in
building a glorious palace.

He taught the unholy demon train to knead
Water and clay, with which, formed into bricks,
The walls were built, and then high turrets, towers,
And balconies, and roofs to keep out rain
And cold and sunshine. Every art was known
To Jemshid, without rival in the world.

CHAPTER III

THE METAPHORS OF THE POETS

" The MYSTIC WORD, clad in poetic dress,
  The shadow is of that proclaimed by Prophet tongue ;
  Majestic strideth PROPHECY in foremost rank,
  While follows humbly in its footsteps POESY. "

ONE of the chief peculiarities of Persian and Ottoman
poetical writings is that they almost always contain,
concealed beneath their literal meaning, an esoteric
and spiritual signification. A certain number of
famous poems, such as, for instance, the Turkish
" *Diwān* of Ashik Pasha," and the Persian " *Mesnevi*
of Jelālū'-d-Dīn, may, indeed, be read for the most
part for what they appear on the surface to be—
religious or moral works. But nearly all the long
Persian romances in verse called *Mesnevi*, the
charming love-stories of *Leyla and Mejnoun*, of
Khusruf and Shirin, of *Yusuf and Zulaikha*,
the *Mantic Uttair*, and many others, are allegorical
representations of the yearning of the soul of man
for union with the Deity, or its love of and quest for
the highest type of spiritual beauty and goodness—
an object attained only when the heart has been
purified by the severest and most painful trials.

The *Ghazels*, or odes, present the same characteristic as the longer poems. Though on the surface
either mere bacchanalian verses or voluptuous love
songs, they are, to those who possess the key to
their symbolic imagery, the fervent outpourings of
hearts ecstasied, or, as they express it, intoxicated

with spiritual love.   For every word in these effusions
has its mystical signification.   It has indeed been
asserted that " every word of Sādi possesses seventy-
two different meanings " ;   and the symbolism of
his verse he himself thus explains :—

Think not, O Khizr, thou favoured of Fortune,
When I of " Wine " sing, the juice of the grape I am
    praising.
" Wine " is to me that which 'bove self exalteth ;
None other ever doth gladden my banquet.
Know that my " Cupbearer " is but of vow the fulfilment ;
" Draught " from the " Tavern " ecstatic oblivion.
Heaven is my witness that long as on earth I have
    sojourned,
Ne'er hath the tip of my lips with the red wine been
    stainèd.

The " Fair One " for whom in these *ghazels* Man,
the " Lover," sighs, is the Deity ;   as is also the
" Loved One " whom he entreats to throw off the
veil that conceals His perfect beauty from view.
The " Ruby Lip " signifies the unspoken, but heard
and understood, words of God ;   " nestling in the
Fair One's tresses " denotes comprehension of the
hidden attributes of the Divinity ;   the " Embrace "
is the revelation to man of the divine mysteries ;
" Separation " or " Absence " from the " Loved
One " is the non-attainment of oneness with the
Deity.   " Wine " is the Divine Love ;   the " Cupbearer " the spiritual instructor, the " giver of the
goblet of celestial aspiration " ;   the " Libertine "
the Saint who has become careless of human conven-
tionalities ;   the " Tavern," a place where one mor-
tifies sensuality, and relinquishes his name and

worldly fame. The " Zephyr " is the breathing of
the Divine Spirit ; the " Taper," the heavenly light
kindling the " Torch," which is the heart of the
Lover, Man ; and so on through every detail. These
ghazels breathe, indeed, in every line a spirit of
ravishment and ecstasy, " picturing the whole
creation as filled with the Divine Love by which
even the most humble plant is excited to seek the
sublime object of its desires." [1]

One of the earliest and most famous of the Dervish
poets was Mohammed ben Ibrahim of Nischapūr,
on whom was conferred the honorific title of Farid-
'd-Dīn (" Pearl of the Faith "), and who was also
known by the soubriquet of " Attar " from his trade
as a perfumer. He was born in 1119, and at the
advanced age of a hundred and ten was massacred
by the Mongols under Yenghiz Khan. One day,
when he was in his shop, a passing Dervish stopped
before him, cast a glance over his wares, and heaved
a deep sigh. Attar, surprised, begged him to go on
his way. " Thou art right," replied the stranger,
" the road to eternity is easy for me ; I have no
encumbrances, for all I possess in the world is my
mantle. Unfortunately it is not so with thee, who
possessest so much valuable merchandise. *But take
heed that thou also prepare thyself for that journey.*"
This advice, according to the biographers, made a
great impression on Attar's mind, and finally caused
him to give up his business and the world in order
to consecrate himself exclusively to the service of

[1] Ubicini, *Letters*, p. 101.

God. For several years he abandoned himself to physical mortifications and religious practices, and subsequently made the pilgrimage to Mekka. He also frequented the society of men famed for eminent piety, and by this means collected the vast store of anecdotes with which he embellished and illustrated his writings, these anecdotes being considered valuable fragments of Moslem biography. In his old age Attar received at Nischapūr the visit of Jelālū-'d-Dīn, to whom he presented a copy of his work, the "*Asrār Nāmā*," or "Book of Secrets," the perusal of which was said to have greatly influenced the younger poet. The most famous of Attar's works is, however, the "*Mantic Uttair*," or "Language of the Birds," a long poem which represents in allegorical form the Soul's Quest for the Divine Love. The Birds had hitherto lived as a Republic, but they felt the necessity of having a King, and took counsel of the Hoopoe who, as she had, according to Moslem legend, accompanied Solomon on his journey to Sheba, was supposed to be the best judge of the qualities requisite in a King. The Hoopoe proposed to them as sovereign the *Sīmorg*, a wonderful bird whose abode was in the Caucasus, and whose excellent qualities she set forth. The birds accept Sīmorg as their King ; but many are dismayed by the dangers of the way and the length of the journey to his abode. A company of Birds finally set out, but the greater number perish by the way of hunger, thirst, or fatigue. At length, after passing through many trials and dangers, thirty survivors

48

only reach the goal of their journey, when they find
in themselves the object of their quest—the *Simorg*,
a word which, in Persian, signifies "thirty birds."
This consummation is thus described by the poet.
When the birds have been introduced by the
Chamberlain into the presence of the Sīmorg :—

They on the Throne of Nearness take their seat
In glory and in majesty's high place,
The Sun of Nearness on them shed His rays,
And, mirrored in each face, these Birds of Earth
Saw the Sīmorg, the Bird of Heaven ;
And when on Him they gazed, but Thirty Birds beheld,
Strange wonderment then fell upon their minds.
Were they still Thirty Birds ? Or were they now Sīmorg ?
They asked themselves, and yet it seemed
That *they* Sīmorg were now, and *He* the Thirty Birds.

    *   *   *   **

Then mutely craved the meaning to be shown
Of this Plurality and Unity combined ;
And, without words, this did Sīmorg reply :
"The Sun that from my majesty rays forth
A mirror is. Whoso approacheth near,
Therein reflected may himself behold,
His body and his soul, himself complete.
Since you as Thirty Birds are hither come,
You in this mirror but those Birds behold.
Thus in my radiance be still lost, absorbed,
That you yourselves may ever find in ME."
The Birds were in Sīmorg thenceforward lost,
As are the sunrays lost within the sun.

The following passage from the same work presents another aspect of the Sūfi doctrines, the
pantheistic conception of Creation. It is addressed
by the spiritually minded Hoopoe to the other
Birds :—

Come ! of this KING admire the handiwork,
Though less than naught it in His eyes appears.

And, as His Essence all the world pervades,
Naught in Creation is, save this alone.
Upon the waters has He fixed His Throne,
This earth suspended in the starry space,
Yet what are seas and what is air ? for all
Is GOD, and but a talisman are heaven and earth
To veil Divinity.   For Heaven and earth,
Did He not permeate them, were but names.
Know then, that both this visible world, and that
Which unseen is, alike are GOD Himself.
Naught is, save GOD ; and all that is, is GOD.
And yet, alas ! by how few is HE seen.
Blind are men's eyes, though all resplendent shines
The world by Deity's own light illumed.
O Thou whom man perceiveth not, although
To him Thou deignest to make known Thyself ;
Thou all Creation art, all we behold, but Thou.
The soul within the body lies concealed,
And Thou dost hide Thyself within the soul.
O soul in soul !   Myst'ry in myst'ry hid !
Before all wert Thou, and art more than all ! [1]

Sādi was a fellow-disciple with Bahā-'d-Dīn [2]
(father of the great poet of Konieh) of the famous
Sheikh Sa'ed-'d-Dīn of Kashgar, [3] who instructed
him in theology and in the principles of Sūfi philosophy ; and in the company of this teacher he
made the first of his fourteen pilgrimages to Mekka.
Sādi was a great traveller.   Besides his Eastern
journeys in Armenia, Arabia, and India, he also
visited Europe, Egypt, and Barbary.   On one
occasion he was captured by the Crusaders and
made to work in the ditch at Tripoli.   From this
slavery he was rescued by a merchant of Aleppo,

[1] See Garcin de Tassy, *Mantic Uttair*.
[2] Mentioned on p. 148
[3] *Ibid*.

who recognised the poet, paid his ransom, and
subsequently gave him his daughter in marriage.
The last thirty years of Sādi's long and adventurous
life—he lived to the great age of a hundred and
sixteen—were spent at Shirāz, a town situated
among charming natural scenery, and blessed with
a delicious climate. Here he wrote the two works
on which his fame chiefly rests, the *Gulistān*,
or " Rosary," and the *Bostān*, or " Garden." The
first consists of prose anecdotes interspersed with
couplets, verses, and moral apologues ; while the
second is entirely a poetical work. The writings of
Sādi are replete with wise proverbial sayings, pious
reflections, and moral precepts, but Sūfi mysticism
also finds a large place in them. In Oriental fashion
he thus addresses himself :—

> Sādi, move thou to Resignation's shrine.
> O man of God, the path of God be thine !
> Hapless is he who from this Haven turns,
> All doors shall spurn him who this Portal spurns.

The tolerance and goodwill to all mankind, irre-
spective of race or creed, so often met with among
the more enlightened Sūfis, formed an admirable
part of Sādi's character, and found expression as
follows :—

> All Adam's race are members of one frame,
> Since all, at first, from the same essence came.
> When, by hard fortune is one limb opprest,
> The other members lose their wonted rest,
> If thou feel not for others' misery,
> A son of Adam is no name for thee.

The *Mesnevi* of Jelālū-'d-Dīn surpasses, in
Oriental estimation, all other works of the kind by

Moslem writers. The word *Mesnevi* signifies at once
the verse-form—a rhymed distich of not less than
twelve couplets—in which romance or epic poetry
is written, and the poem itself ; and the work of
the poet of Konieh is by common consent termed
simply *The Mesnevi*, or " Poem of Poems." Like
all the early Dervish literature, it is in Persian, and
consists of a number of pieces written in the form of
apologues, with digressions on Sūfi doctrines. The
work is divided into six Books or Parts, and contains
twenty-six thousand six hundred and sixty couplets. [1]
Like his forerunner, Sādi, the great founder of the
Mevlevi Order preaches tolerance and large-minded-
ness, as in the following charming parable which I
give in Mr. Whinfield's prose translation :—

" Moses once heard a shepherd praying as follows :
' O God, show me where Thou art that I may become
Thy servant. I will clean Thy shoes, and comb Thy
hair, and sew Thy clothes, and fetch Thee milk.'
When Moses heard him praying in this senseless
manner, he rebuked him, saying, ' O foolish one,

[1] Portions only of the *Mesnevi* have, so far as my knowledge goes, as yet been translated into any European
language. The late Sir James Redhouse published in
Trubner's *Oriental Series* a volume containing translations
of a number of pieces from the First Book of that work.
The renderings of the late Orientalist are, however, often
grotesque in their exceeding baldness ; while comparison
with Mr. Whinfield's literal prose translations of the same
passages makes it evident that, in order to meet the exi-
gencies of rhyme and metre, many words and phrases have
been added which completely obscure the sense of the
original lines.

though your father was a Moslem, you have become
an infidel ! God is a spirit, and needs not such gross
ministrations as in your ignorance you suppose.'
The shepherd was abashed at the Prophet's rebuke ;
he tore his clothes and fled away into the desert.
Then a voice from heaven was heard, saying, ' O
Moses, wherefore hast thou driven away My servant ?
Thine office it is to reconcile my people with Me, not
to drive them away from Me. I have given to
men different usages and forms of praising and of
adoring Me. I have no need of their praises, being
exalted high above all such needs. I regard not
the words which are spoken, but the heart that
offers them.' "

The following poem, which forms a kind of Pro-
logue to the *Mesnevi*, was translated a century
ago by the celebrated Orientalist, Sir William
Jones :— [1]

SONG OF THE REED-FLUTE [2]

Hear how yon reed, in sadly pleasing tales,
Departed bliss and present woe bewails :
" With me, from native banks untimely torn,
Love-warbling youths and soft-eyed virgins mourn.
O ! let the heart by fatal absence rent,
Feel what I sing, and bleed when I lament :
Who roams in exile from his parent bower,
Pants to return, and chides each lingering hour.
My notes in circles of the grave and gay,
Have hailed the rising, cheered the closing day.
Each in my fond affections claimed a part,
But none discerned the secret of my heart.

[1] *The Works*, Vol. I.
[2] See p. 110. *The Mystic Reed-flute.*

What though my strains and sorrows slow combined,
Yet ears are dull, and carnal eyes are blind.
Free through each mortal form the spirits roll,
But sighs avail not. Can we see the soul ? "

Such notes breathed gently from yon vocal frame.
Breathed, said I ? No ! 'Twas all enlivening flame.
'Tis love that fills the reed with warmth divine ;
'Tis love that sparkles in the rosy wine.
The plaintive wand'rer from my peerless maid,
The reed has fired, and all my soul betrayed.
He gives the bane and he with balsam cures ;
Afflicts, yet soothes, impassions, yet allures.
Hail, heavenly Love ! true source of endless gains !
Thy balm restores me, and thy skill sustains.
O more than Galen learned, than Plato wise,
My guide, my law, my joy supreme, arise !
Love warms this frigid clay with mystic fire,
And dancing mountains leap with young desire.
Blest is the soul that swims in seas of love,
And long the life sustained by food above.
With forms imperfect can perfection dwell ?
Here pause, my song ; and thou, vain world, farewell !

The following charming little parable, so
essentially Sūfi in spirit, is already a favourite
with Europeans.   It is from " The Lion's Hunt " :—

A Dervish once to his Friend's door drew nigh, and knocked.
" Who art thou, Faithful One ? " was asked, ere 'twas
    unlocked.
" 'Tis I," the Dervish cried.   " Then in thou mayst not
    come ;
For at my well-dressed feast there is for raw no room,"
Replied the Friend.   " But separation's fiery smart
Can purify the crude, and cleanse from guile his heart.
Since from the bonds of self thou art not yet set free,
By fiery flame alone canst thou refinèd be."
The Dervish went away.   For one whole weary year
Did wander, grief-consumed, his Friend no longer near.

Then, cleansed at length by fire till self became as naught,
He turned him back again ; his Friend's abode he sought,
And at His door he knocked, with trembling hand and
  meek,
Fearing some careless word his foolish lips might speak.
Again then asked the Friend : "Who at my door knocks
  low ? "
He answered only, "O Belov'd, Belov'd, 'tis thou ! "
" Since 'tis Myself that knocks, the door stands open wide—
But could two I's beneath one roof in peace abide ? "[1]

The following passage, also from the *Mesnevi*,
refers to the Dervish *Pir*, Bayazid Bestemi, mentioned in the first chapter, and interestingly illustrates the Sūfi doctrine of union with the Deity.
When on his pilgrimage to Mekka, Bayazid visited
all the " Pillars of Insight " who had their abodes
in the various towns through which he had to pass.
One day he had the happiness to discover the
" Axis,"[2] or greatest saint of the time, in the
person of a venerable Dervish with whom he held
the following conversation :—

" Say now, O Bayazid, to what town art thou bound,
Where will thy weary caravan its rest have found ? "
" At dawn I to the holy Ka'aba[3] take my way."
" But how wilt thou the cost of that long journey pay ? "
" Two hundred silver *dirhems* do I bear with me,
Sewn in the corner of my cloak for safety, see ! "
" Walk sev'n times round *me*, Bayazid," the Sage then said.
" Greater thy gain than hadst the Ka'aba's circuit made !
As for thy *dirhems*, liberal one, give them to me,
For now thy journey's o'er, thou thy desire dost see.
Thy Pilgrimage is made, Eternal Life hast gained,
Heav'n's purity in one brief moment hast attained.

[1] Versified from Mr. Whinfield's prose translation.
[2] See p. 32.
[3] The Sanctuary at Mekka.

That which thy soul in me doth see is truly God,
For He hath chosen me to make me His abode.
Unto the Ka'aba He His Grace and Favour shows,
But to my body He HIS SECRET doth disclose.
Hath He, since He that house built, e'en to enter deigned ?
But, save th' Eternal One, none entrance here hath gained.
When Thou hast *me* beheld, then Allah hast thou seen,
And round about the holy Ka'aba thou hast been.
Thou servest *me*, and Allah worshipped is, and praised ;
For think not He so high above all men is raised.
Thy mind's eye open wide, and fix thou it on *me*
That, in a mortal, Thou the Light of God mayst see.
Once only the Belov'd ' My House ' the Ka'aba named,
But *me* He seventy times has as ' His Servant ' [1] claimed.
O happy Bayazid, thou hast the Ka'aba found,
And now art with a thousand precious blessings crowned ! "

Jelālū-'d-Dīn also left behind him a large collec-
tion of *ghazels*, or odes.   This is a verse-form which
may contain from three to twenty-five distichs, the
two first lines rhyming with the second line of each
succeeding couplet.   This peculiarity of rhyme has,
however, been disregarded in the following *ghazels*,
translated by Professor Falconer, but may be
remarked in Mr. Gibb's renderings of *ghazels* by
Ottoman poets :—

All earthly forms, where beauty dwells enshrined,
That beauty borrow from the Infinite mind,
Why grieve we when the faint reflections fade ?—
Their source and prototype are undecayed.

The form whose beauty woos the raptured eye,
The strain that steeps the soul in ecstasy,
When *that* hath vanished, and *this* ceased to flow,
Why weep and call it death, which seems but so ?

[1] Alluding to a passage in the *Hadis* or Traditions,
which says, " Heaven and earth cannot contain me, but the
heart of my faithful Servant containeth me ! "

Long as the gushing fount its circle fills,
Can it forget to feed its thousand rills ?
Thy soul a fount is—thoughts, shapes, sounds of earth
Flow thence, as rivers from their source have birth.

See, to what precious metal is refined
Ignoble dust, when linked to godlike mind ;
Nor doubt when thou hast filled thy part as man,
Angel awaits thee in the mighty plan,
With starry heaven thy home—a bright abode,
Far from the spot thy mortal footsteps trode.

Nor yet at Angel shall thy being's motion
Be stayed, but onward press to Being's ocean.
There shall thy atom-drop become a sea,
Vast as a hundred deeps, wide, weltering, boundless, free,
Then boldly, son, proclaim in faith and truth,
This creed : *Though forms decay, souls own a deathless youth.*

Passing on to the fifteenth century, we come to
Jāmī, who was born in the year 1414 at the town
of Jām in Khorassan, from which he took his pen-
name. To his real name of Abdul-rahman was
added that of Nūr-'d-Dīn (" Light of the Faith "),
and in later years his fame for learning and sanctity
gained also for him that of *Mevlana* (" Our Lord "
or " Master "). Jāmi left behind him at least fifty
volumes of poetry, grammar, and theology, which
are still read and admired in the Eastern world.
Seven of his best mystical poems are called *The
Seven Thrones*, but the most famous of all is his
Yusuf and Zulaikha, considered by European
authorities to be one of the finest compositions in
the Persian language.[1] Of the following passages
the first and second are taken from the introductory,

[1] See *Preface* to Rozenzweig's translation of *Yusuf and
Zulaikha*, also his *Analysis* and Specimens of the *Joseph and
Zulaikha*, 1872. Griffith, *Yusuf and Zulaikha*, 1882.

and the third from one of the concluding cantos of
this poem. In this touching story of the loves of
Joseph and " Potiphar's Wife " is symbolised the
yearning of the human soul for the highest moral
beauty and perfection :—

(I)

In solitude, where Being signless dwelt,
And all the Universe still dormant lay
Concealed in selfishness, One Being was
Exempt from " I-" or " Thou "-ness, and apart
From all duality ; Beauty Supreme,
Unmanifest, except unto itself
By its own light, yet fraught with power to charm
The souls of all ; concealed in the Unseen,
An essence pure, unstained by aught of ill.
No mirror to reflect Its loveliness,
Nor comb to touch Its locks ; the morning breeze
Ne'er stirred Its tresses ; no collyrium
Lent lustre to Its eyes ; no rosy cheeks
O'ershadowed by dark curls like hyacinth,
Nor peach-like down were there ; no dusky mole
Adorned Its face ; no eye had yet beheld
Its image. To Itself it sang of love
In wordless measures. By Itself it cast
The die of love.
               But Beauty cannot brook
Concealment and the veil, nor patient rest
Unseen and unadmired : 'twill burst all bonds,
And from Its prison casement to the world
Reveal Itself. See where the tulip grows
In upland meadows, how in balmy spring
It decks itself ; and how amidst its thorns,
The wild rose rends its garment, and reveals
Its loveliness. Thou, too, when some rare thought
Or beauteous image, or deep mystery
Flashes across thy soul, canst not endure
To let it pass, but hold'st it, that perchance
In speech or writing thou may'st send it forth
To charm the world.

                              Wherever Beauty dwells
Such is its nature, and its heritage
From Everlasting Beauty, which emerged
From realms of purity to shine upon
The worlds, and all the souls that dwell therein.
One gleam fell from It on the Universe
And on the angels, and this single ray
Dazzled the angels till their senses whirled
Like the revolving sky.   In divers forms
Each mirror showed It forth, and everywhere
Its praise was chanted in new harmonies.

               *   *   *   *   *

Each speck of matter did He constitute
A mirror, causing each one to reflect
The beauty of His visage.   From the rose
Flashed forth His beauty, and the nightingale,
Beholding it, loved madly.   From that Light
The candle drew the lustre which beguiles
The moth to immolation.   On the sun
His Beauty shone, and straightway from the wave
The lotus reared its head.   Each shining lock
Of Leyla's hair attracted Mejuūn's heart
Because some ray divine reflected shone
In her fair face.   'Twas He to Shirin's lips
Who lent that sweetness which had power to steal
The heart from Parviz, and from Ferhad life.

His Beauty everywhere doth show itself,
And through the forms of earthly beauties shines
Obscured, as through a veil.   He did reveal
His face through Joseph's coat, and so destroyed
Zuleykha's peace.   Where'er thou seest a veil,
Beneath that veil He hides.   Whatever heart
Doth yield to love, He charms it.   In His love
The heart hath life.   Longing for Him, the soul
Hath victory.   That heart which feigns to love
The fair ones of this world, loves Him alone.
Beware ! say not " He is All-Beautiful,
And we His lovers."   Thou art but the glass,
And He the Face [1] confronting it, which casts

     [1] "All things shall perish save His Face."   *Koran*
xxviii. 88.

Its image on the mirror. He alone
Is manifest, and thou in truth art hid.
Pure Love, like Beauty, coming but from Him
Reveals itself in Thee. If steadfastly
Thou canst regard, thou wilt at length perceive
He is the mirror also—He alike
The Treasure and the Casket. " I " and " Thou "
Have here no place, and are but phantasies
Vain and unreal. Silence ! for this tale
Is endless, and no eloquence hath power
To speak of Him. 'Tis best for us to love
And suffer silently, being as naught.[1]

(II)

No heart is that which Love ne'er wounded ; they
Who know not lover's pangs are soulless clay.
Turn from the world, O turn thy wandering feet ;
Come to the World of Love and find it sweet !
Heaven's giddy round from craze of love was caught,
From Love's disputes the world with strife is fraught.
Love's slave be thou if thou would fain be free :
Welcome love's pangs, and happy shalt thou be.

Love's sweet, soft memories youth itself restore ;
The tale of love gives fame for evermore.
If Majuūn ne'er the cup of love had drained,
High fame in heaven and earth he ne'er had gained.
A thousand sages, deep in wisdom's lore,
Untaught of Love, died, and are known no more :
Without a name or trace in death they sank,
And in the book of time their name is blank.[2]

The following dialogue occurs between Yusuf and
Zulaikha on meeting after a long separation, during
which her husband, the Wazir of Egypt, has
died, and she has become poor and blind. This

[1] Translated by Mr. R. T. H. Browne in *A Year Among
the Persians*, pp. 125-7.
[2] Griffith, *Yusuf and Zulaikha*, p. 23.

"separation" of course symbolises the estrange-
ment of the human heart from the Divine
Love :—

"Where are thy youth, and thy beauty, and pride ? "
"Gone, since I parted from thee," she replied.
"Where is the light of thine eyes ? " said he.
"Drowned in blood-tears for the loss of thee."
"Why is that cypress-tree[1] bowed and bent ? "
"By absence from thee and my long lament."
"Where are thy pearls and thy silver and gold ?
And the diadem bright on thy head of old ? "
"They who spoke of my loved one," she answered, "shed,
In the praise of his beauty, rare pearls on my head.
In return for those jewels, a recompense meet,
I scattered my jewels and gold at their feet.
My crown of pure gold on their foreheads I set,
And the dust that they trod made my coronet.
I gave till the stream of my treasure ran dry,
My heart is Love's storehouse, and I am I."[2]

Not in the Persian language alone, however, has
poetical utterance been given to the mystical
doctrines of the Dervishes. From the first half of
the fourteenth century onward this language began
to be abandoned for literary purposes by Ottomans
in favour of their native Turkish. Though both
the prose and verse productions in that language,
previous to the end of the following century, are
adjudged by critics to be for the most part somewhat
rude and uncouth, one of the earliest of these
Turkish writers was of such eminence that he is to
this day styled the "Father of Ottoman Literature."

[1] The human form is often likened to a cypress by
Oriental poets, and also by the Greek popular muse.
[2] Griffith, *Yusuf and Zulaikha*, pp. 293-4.

Oriental writers have always affected anonymity, and this author wrote under the *takhullus*, or pen-name of A'ashik ("The Loving") to which name, according to the custom of those times, was added the title of "Pasha" to denote his high rank among men of letters. Among A'ashik's numerous productions is an "Ode to Culture"; but he was chiefly eminent as a mystic, having been a member of the *Mevlevi* Order, and his principal work is a long mystical poem known as the "*A'ashik Pasha Diwāni*." It consists of rhymed couplets, the following translated lines from which may give some idea of the character and sentiment of the Turkish poetry of that period :—

> All the Universe, one mighty sign, is shown ;
> God hath myriads of creative acts unknown :
> None hath seen them, of the races *djin*[1] and men,
> None hath news brought from that realm far off from ken,
> Never shall thy mind in reason reach that strand,
> Nor can tongue the King's name utter of that land.
> Since 'tis His each nothingness with life to invest,
> Trouble is there ne'er at His behest.
> Eighteen thousand worlds from end to end
> Do not with Him one atom's worth transcend.[2]

Khiyāli lived in the first half of the sixteenth century. He began life as a Kalender of the School of Ali Baba, but on coming to the capital he found a patron in the Grand Vizier, who introduced him to the notice of the Sultan.

---

[1] The race of beings created, according to Moslem tradition, before Adam.

[2] Translated by Mr. Gibb in his *Ottoman Poems*.

GHAZEL

One with Realms Eternal this my soul to make—what
   wouldest say ?
All Creation's empire's fancies to forsake—what wouldest
   say ?
Wearing to a hair my frame with bitter sighs and moans,
   in love,
Nestling in The Fair One's tresses, to rest take—what
   wouldest say ?
Yonder goldfaced birds within the quicksilver resplendent
   deep :
Launching forth the hawk, my striving, these to take—
   what wouldest say ?
Yonder Nine Smaragdine Bowls of Heaven to quaff at
   one deep draught,
Yet from all ebriety's fumes free to break—what wouldest
   say ?
To an autumn leaf the Sphere hath turned Khiyali's
   countenance,
To the Spring of Beauty, that a gift to make—what
   wouldest say ? [1]

Many more examples might be given, did space
allow, from the mystic poetry of Sheykhi, Lami,
Yahya Bey, and other later writers. This chapter
must, however, conclude with a *ghazel* of Sidqi, the
famous Ottoman poetess of the seventeenth century,
a prolific writer, whose works are full of Sūfi
mysticism :— [2]

He who union with the Lord gains, more desireth not ;
He who looks on charms of Fair One, other sight desireth
   not ;
Pang of love is lover's solace, eagerly he seeks therefor,
Joys he in it ; balm or salve for yonder blight desireth
   not.

[1] Gibb, *Ottoman Poems*.
[2] See my *Women of Turkey*, Vol. II, Chap. xxiv.
"Poetesses of the Rise, Decline, and Fall of the Ottoman
Empire."

Paradise he longs not after, nor doth aught beside regard,
Bower, or garden, mead, or youth or *Hūri* bright desireth
    not.
From the hand of Power Unbounded, draweth he the
    wine of life ;
Aye inebriate with knowledge, learning's light desireth
    not.
He who Allah loveth, Lord is of an empire, such that he—
King of inward mysteries—Suleymān's might desireth
    not :
Thou art Sultan of my heart, ay, soul of my soul e'en
    art Thou ;
Thou art soul enow, and Sidqī other plight desireth not. [1]

[1] Gibb, *Ottoman Poems*.

CHAPTER IV

MONASTERIES AND SHRINES

" If your hearts be oppressed with sorrow, go seek consolation at the graves of the holy dead."—*Traditional
saying of Mohammed.*

THE monastic establishments of the Dervish Orders,
called by the various names of *Tekkehs*, *Khānakāhs*,
and *Zanriyehs*, but more commonly by the first,
and the *Turbehs*, or Shrines of their Saints, are, at
the present day, as numerous in European as in
Asiatic Turkey.   In Constantinople and its environs
many of the Orders possess several establishments ;
and every town contains the monastery and shrine
of one or more of their communities.   The *Tekkehs*
occupy for the most part picturesque and commanding situations, sometimes in the middle of towns or
cities, but more frequently in their suburbs.   Those
of the *Mevlevi* and *Rufai* are perhaps the most
remarkable.   The central edifice of the former is
the *Sem'a Khaneh* (" The Hall of Celestial Sounds "),
where the Brotherhood meet for the performance
of their religious exercises and public worship.   This
is usually a square building of whitewashed masonry,
with a domed and red-tiled roof.   The interior
arrangements vary somewhat, but are always
marked by the utmost simplicity.   A circular space
in the centre is smoothly planked and reserved for
the performances of the Dervishes.   It is divided

by a low wooden railing from the rest of the floor, which is covered with matting and occupied during the public services by the male spectators. A gallery, supported on wooden pillars, runs round three sides of the *Tekkeh ;* one side of it is occupied by the *Mutrib,* or orchestra, and the other two by the women and children, who are concealed from view by carved lattices. In some *Tekkehs,* where the gallery is only large enough to accommodate the orchestra, a corner of the ground floor is partitioned off for the women. The only attempts at decoration are tablets on the walls inscribed with texts from the Koran, and with the names of Allah, Mohammed, Ali, and Hasan and Husein, the grandsons of the Prophet. As in the public mosques, the direction of Mekka is indicated by a niche in the wall, surmounted by the name of the *Pir,* or Founder of the Order, and sometimes also by the Moslem profession of faith—*La ilaha il Allah ve Mohammed resoul Allah* (" There is no god but Allah and Mohammed is the Prophet of Allah "), or the word *Bismillah* (" In the Name of Allah "). In a corner of many *Tekkehs* is the shrine of a departed saintly sheikh, covered with costly carpets and rich draperies, the pious offerings of those who have there sought and found healing benefit, or other boon.

The *Tekkehs* of the *Mevlevi* Order contain another apartment called the *Ismi Jeleeh Hūjreh,* where the Brethren perform their daily *namāz* and the obligatory *zikr,* or calling upon the name of Allah, which takes place at the hour of the third *namāz.* The

courtyard surrounding the *Tekkeh* gives access to
the cells of the monastic Dervishes and their Sheikh.
These are, in a fully-equipped monastery, eighteen
in number, and form a quadrangle of low buildings,
with a roof sloping to the front, and covering a
broad verandah into which all the doors and windows
open. Beyond are flower and fruit gardens, shaded
by cypress, mulberry, and plane trees, the haunts
of storks and pigeons ; and, enclosed by the arched
gateway and tile-topped walls, are cisterns and
fountains of sparkling water furnished with iron
ladles for the use of the thirsty. Sometimes, as
within the precincts of the *Tekkeh* outside the
Vardar gate of Salonica, there are also cool, shady
cloisters and raised terraces and kiosks, commanding
magnificent views of mountain, plain, and sea.
And here, when the evening shadows are lengthening,
the mystics, in their picturesque and symbolic
attire, may be seen pacing tranquilly to and fro ;
or, seated on the broad wooden benches, medita-
tively passing through their fingers the brown beads
of their long *tesbehs*, or rosaries, on their faces
that expression of perfect repose which indifference
to the world and its doings alone can give.

Though all the Dervish Orders, in accordance
with their principle of Poverty, are considered
mendicant, few are so in reality, for most *Tekkehs*
possess *vakouf*, or landed property bequeathed to
them by pious persons. The revenues from these
endowments are applied chiefly to the support of
the monastic Dervishes, though the wants of a

needy lay brother may occasionally be relieved from them. The *Tekkehs* vary greatly in point of wealth, and the more prosperous are expected to assist others less largely endowed. The *Mevlevi* Order is the most popular, one might even say the most fashionable, of all, and has, ever since its foundation, included among its members men of high rank. The late Sultan Abdul Aziz was, for instance, a lay Brother, and occasionally, it is said, took part in the religious exercises at one of the *Mevlevi Tekkehs* in Constantinople. This Order is, consequently, very prosperous, and its monasteries and shrines surpass those of all other Orders. The Monastery of its General, at Konieh (Iconium), in Asia Minor, possesses considerable lands bequeathed as *vakouf* by the old Seljukian Sultans, these bequests being ratified by subsequent princes. Murad IV, too, when marching against Persia in 1634, bestowed many favours and distinctions upon the " Sheikh of Sheikhs," as their Grand Master is termed, and endowed his community as a perpetual *vakouf* with the proceeds of the *kharatch*, the poll-tax imposed on the non-Moslem inhabitants of the city in lieu of military service, now abolished.

Notwithstanding, however, these substantial endowments, the Dervishes have never, like the monastic Orders of Christendom, departed from the original principles of their founders. Their manner of living is still as frugal as was that of the original Twelve Orders, and the architecture of their *Tekkehs* is marked by extreme simplicity

both of form and material, any ornamental articles
they may contain being the gifts of the pious ; while
their surplus revenues are either given directly to
the poor in the shape of alms, or employed in the
foundation of charitable institutions such as
almshouses, schools, or baths.

When it happens that a Dervish has been raised
to the rank of Sheikh by the General of his Order,
without being appointed to the rule of a special
Tekkeh, he is directed to take up his abode in some
town which has been indicated to his Chief, by
means of a dream or vision, as specially marked out
for the establishment of a new community. Here
he remains until the citizens, incited by a pious
emulation, erect a *Tekkeh* and provide for its support. Most of the existing monasteries have sprung
up in this way ; and the practice, to some extent,
still continues.

It is not unusual to find *Mevlevi* Sheikhs engaged
in commercial pursuits, necessitated by the nature
of the source from which their revenues are derived.
For instance, if the *vakouf* consists of arable land,
and is cultivated on the *metayer* system, the sale
of the produce devolves on the Sheikh, who generally
proves himself well able to fulfil the temporal, as
well as the spiritual, duties of his office. I happened one day, after witnessing a performance of
the *Mevlevi* Dervishes at Salonica, to make a
remark to the Inspector of Customs on the pre-
possessing appearance and reverend bearing of the
Sheikh, a handsome man in the prime of life. " Oh,"

he replied, laughing, " Ne vous fiez pas à sa bonne physionomie ; il n'y a personne qui me donne plus d'embarras dans les affaires." But even St. Theresa, it appears, was a very good business woman.[1]

The great founder of this Order, to judge from the following anecdote, also knew how to turn his position to account for the advantage of his community :—

" Whenever the grandees of Konieh entertained a desire to have an audience of the Sheikh Shemsu 'd-Dīn of Tebriz, they would request Husām (Jelāl's secretary) to procure it for them through the influence of his master with the Sheikh. Jelāl and Husām used to tax those nobles for this favour according to their means and circumstances. On one occasion the Grand Vizier solicited an audience, and was taxed at forty thousand pieces of silver ; which sum, after much chaffering, was reduced to thirty thousand. At his audience with Shems, the Vizier was so charmed with the mysteries revealed to him that, on his return therefrom, he voluntarily sent to Husām the ten thousand pieces of silver which had been abated from the sum originally fixed. These moneys were always expended by Husām as he saw fit, in relieving the necessities of the holy community, and the families of Jelāl, the gold-beater (Husām), and their various dependents."[2]

[1] See Mrs. Cunningham Graham's *Life of St. Theresa*, 1894.
[2] *The Acts of the Adepts.* Sir W. Redhouse's Translation.

The *Tekkehs* of the Bektāshīs are unostentatious
groups of buildings, consisting of cells for the
brethren and a plain square hall for their common
devotions. In the centre of the floor is a large
dodecangular stone called the *Maidan Tāsh*, on
which, during all their ceremonies except that of
initiation, stands a lighted candle. Around this
are twelve *postakis*, or sheepskin mats, significative
of the twelve *Imāms ;* the one nearest to a niche in
the wall which denotes the *Kibleh*, or direction of
Mekka, being the seat of the Sheikh, and the others
those of the eleven elders. The apartment reserved
for the Sheikh is called the " cell of the master."
He, however, unless under a vow of celibacy, seldom
occupies it permanently, but resides with his family ;
and the rule of the convent in his absence devolves
upon a deputy Sheikh, the senior of the celibates.
Those of the Orders who for various reasons
are, like the Hamzavis, under the ban of the ruling
powers, assemble in buildings undistinguishable
externally from ordinary dwelling-houses.

The tombs of the *Evliya*, as Moslem saints are
called, are held in religious veneration in all Mohammedan countries, and are honoured by the erection
over them of *Turbéhs*, or mausoleums. A *Turbéh*
is usually a square edifice with a domed roof built
over a sarcophagus of stone or brickwork, higher at
the head than at the foot and rising in the centre
to a ridge. To some *Turbéhs* are attached apart-
ments in which reside the Dervishes who have
charge of them. The walls of these shrines have

grated openings through which can be seen the tomb, often covered with rich shawls and carpets, the pious offerings of recipients of benefits believed to have been bestowed through the mediation of the Saint buried there. On the gratings flutter innumerable little coloured rags, portions of the clothing of rich persons who hope by this means to transfer their diseases to the Saint, or who leave them as *votive tabellæ* to remind him of the blessings hoped for through his mediation with Allah. In a niche in the masonry of the sarcophagus a small lamp, fed with sweet oil, is kept continually burning. These lamps symbolise the *nūr*, or holy light, which, it is said, is frequently seen to hover over the grave of a Saint, and has made known the resting-place of many holy Dervishes who have died while on journeys or pilgrimages.

Among the famous Sheikhs who held the post of guardian of a shrine was the *Pir*, Abdūl Kadr Ghilāni, the founder of the Kadiri Order.[1] He had charge of the tomb of the celebrated Imām, Abū Khanife, at Bagdad, where he also was buried. And round the *Turbéh* of Abdūl Kadr ("The Rose of Bagdad") are grouped in such numbers the domes that cover the mortal remains of the most renowned mystics of the East that the locality is known to the present day as "The Grove of the Saints."

The *Turbéh* at Broussa of the famous Dervish, Emir Sultan,[2] is thus described by Evliya Effendi,

[1] See p. 18.   [2] See p. 33.

who visited it towards the end of the seventeenth century. [1]

"He is buried without Broussa to the east, beneath a lofty dome. The gates of the *Turbéh* are inlaid with silver, as also is the entrance, at which the visitor descends six steps. The walls are covered with variegated porcelain tiles. Four of the windows look westwards towards the plain of Broussa, and four towards the Kibleh (Mekka) into the yard of the *Turbéh*. The great number of suspended ornaments which adorn the interior of the mausoleum are equalled only in the *Turbéhs* of Medina ; the silken carpets are richer than are found anywhere else. The sarcophagus is surrounded by gold and silver lamps, candlesticks, and vases for holding perfumes and rosewater ; on the richly-embroidered silken draperies which cover it lie Korans writ by the hands of famous scribes ; [2] and at the head a large turban stands majestically. Those who enter are struck with such awe that many do not dare to attempt it, but only look into it by a window at the head, and recite a *Fatiha*." [3]

[1] *Narrative of Travels.*

[2] Though printing was introduced into Turkey more than a century and a half ago, a beautiful manuscript is at the present day preferred to a printed book, and many beautifully written and illuminated copies of the Koran are to be found in the country, as a prejudice still exists against printing the Sacred Book.

[3] The first chapter of the Koran, the Moslem *Paternoster.* "Mohammedans look upon the *Fatiha* as the quintessence of the whole Koran, and often repeat it in their devotions both public and private." Sale, *Al Koran*, p. 1, note.

A village called Bektāshkeui, near Angora, contains the tomb of Hadji Bektāsh, the founder of the Bektāshi Order. It stands in a commanding position overlooking the city, under the dome of a *Turbéh*, and close by is a *Tekkeh* occupied by a small community of Bektāshi Dervishes. This shrine is naturally much venerated, and visited by pilgrims from all parts of the Empire. The front of the *Tekkeh* is embellished with a portico or verandah, supported on pillars of marble, and on the side of a well in the court visitors are shown indentations said to have been made by the teeth of the Saint, and in the doorway the impression of his hand. In the vicinity are salt mines which, tradition says, were miraculously created by Hadji Bektāsh, who, when passing through the village, had found the inhabitants suffering from a scarcity of that commodity. This village now bears the name of Touzkeui, the "Salt Village."

At Merdevenkeui, a village not far from the Asiatic suburb of Kadikeui, is the *Turbéh* of an eminent Bektāshi saint, once a *Chaoush*, or messenger in the service of Sultan Achmet, which is much frequented by pious Moslems. Close by is a large stone said to possess the power of granting the wish of any person standing upon it. A Turkish lady of my acquaintance, the late Besmi Sultana, attributed her elevation to the high and exceptional position of legal wife of Sultan Abdul Medjid to the wish she mentally expressed when standing on this

stone, after, of course, depositing her devotional
offering on the neighbouring shrine of the
Evliyā.

Many *Turbéhs*, however, consist merely of four
roofless walls, pierced with grated openings, built
round the sarcophagus. Some are to be found in
the crowded thoroughfares of towns and cities,
some by country roadsides, while others occupy
corners of the public burial grounds. At Salonica,
one is situated at the entrance to the bazaar, and
another curiously located in the cellar basement of
a Jewish merchant's warehouse, the tomb being
visible from the street through a grated opening
close to the ground. The cost of the lights always
kept burning in these humbler shrines is defrayed
either by some pious bequest, or by the offerings of
the passers-by.

It is customary for a visitor, or pilgrim, on arriving
at a *turbéh*, to greet its saintly occupant as he would
a living person with the beautiful Oriental salutation, " Peace be with you " (*Salaam aleikūm*). He
then recites a *Fatiha*[1] before the entrance, and,
walking round the grave from left to right, repeats
it at each of the four sides. Sometimes a longer
sura of the Koran is used, or, perhaps, as in the case
of a devout Dervish on his pilgrimage, the whole of
the Sacred Book. The recitation concludes with
this collect, apparently addressed to the Saint :
" Extol the perfection of thy Lord, the Lord of
might, exempting Him from that which they

[1] See above, p. 72.

[Christians] ascribe to Him " [*i.e.* having a partaker of his Godhead].

These arts of devotion are generally performed for the sake of the Saint, though the merit of them is also believed to reflect at the same time upon the pilgrim who makes the recitation, and adds the words " Peace be upon the Apostles and praise be to Allah, the Lord of all creatures. O Allah ! I have transferred the merit of what I have recited from the excellent Koran to the soul of this Saint." When prayers are offered for some special blessing—which usually, if not for health or deliverance from some impending calamity, is of a purely worldly nature, such as the furtherance of some ambitious project, or the favour of the Sultan, or some other dignitary whose influence is required—the following, or some similar formula, is used : " O Allah ! I conjure Thee by the Prophet, and by him to whom this place is dedicated, to grant me," etc. The hands of the suppliant are held upwards and open during the prayer, and, at its conclusion, passed over the face. Some fervent pilgrims, like Evliya Effendi, kiss the threshold, others the walls, windows, and grave-coverings of the holy shrines.

The prayers of the guardians of *Turbéhs* are also often solicited by those in need of spiritual consolation and assistance. These watchers of the holy dead are often Sheikhs who have abandoned the world for this purpose, and whose lives of undoubted purity exalt them to the position of intermediaries between the Saint and ordinary sinful men. They have often one or more disciples to assist them in their pious duties, who in due time succeed their spiritual guide in his office. The revenues are derived chiefly from the offerings of pilgrims, but in some cases *turbéhs*, like *tekkehs*, are endowed with landed property.

The tombs of Christian saints, strange to say, come in for their share of the general hagiolatry, though, as the Christians also patronise Moslem saints, this is but a *quid pro quo*. The beautiful basilica of St. Dimitri at Salonica, built in the fifth century over the miracle-working tomb of that Saint, was, in 1180, for the second time, converted into a mosque. On the removal of the ʿΑγία Τράπεζα —the Holy Table of the Greek Church—the relics which had had their resting-place beneath it were reverently removed to a cell at the north-west corner of the narthex. The Greeks and other Christians are now allowed to visit this shrine freely ; and the old *Mevlevi* Dervish, who acts as caretaker of the mosque, appears to have no less faith in the miraculous powers of St. Dimitri than have the numerous members of the Orthodox Church who make pilgrimages to his shrine. One of my visits to this ancient Metropolitan Church was paid in company with a Greek matron who, having been educated in Germany and France, was a thorough sceptic in such matters. Seeing that we were strangers, the Dervish enumerated in his broken Greek the virtues and antiquity of the Saint. He then fumbled under the tombstone and produced a handful of

earth and what looked like a long mesh of cotton
candlewick. Having ascertained from my friend
her name, and the names of her husband, father-
in-law, and children, the old man slowly repeated
them, tying at each name a knot in the cotton
over the flame of the candle burning on the tomb,
and then presented her with this girdle with the
assurance that, if worn on the person it would
relieve her or them of any of the ills to which the
flesh is heir. I was also the fortunate recipient of
a small quantity of greasy earth, from which I was
promised similar benefits.[1]

[1] An odoriferous unguent (μύρον) is said to exude
from the bones of certain saints who from this circumstance
are called μυροβλύται. St. Nicholas is one of these
myroblites. Sir John Maunderville, speaking of the relics
of St. Catharine, on Mount Sinai, says, " The prelate of the
Monkes schewethe the Relykes to the Pilgrymes. And
with an Instrument of Sylver, he frotethe the Bones : and
thanne ther gothe out a lytylle Oyle, as thoughe it were in
a maner swetynge, that is nouther like to Oyle ne to
Bawme ; but it is fulle swete of smelle." (Quoted by
Mr. Athelstan Riley in *Mount Athos*, p. 127 n.)

CHAPTER V

MONASTIC RULE AND DISCIPLINE

" Who Poverty's low door to enter e'er has sought,
    Aye to his death beneath its roof remains,
Lays greed aside, and, as a monarch reigns ;
    For proud the station is of him who needeth naught."

A DERVISH *Tekkeh*, or convent, usually contains
from fifteen to thirty disciples, ruled over by a
Sheikh. The Sheikh has unlimited power and
authority in the *Tekkeh*. If it is endowed with
vakouf property, he sells the produce of the farms,
regulates the expenditure of the *Tekkeh*, and distributes its alms. If his convent is unendowed, he
looks for its support to the pious and charitable—
the " Friends of Allah." For, occupied as he is
supposed continually to be with spiritual matters,
a Sheikh cannot, like his disciples, follow a worldly
avocation, but must live—according to the Dervish
expression—" on the Doorstep of Allah." The disciples are also expected to contribute to his support
and to the other expenses of the *Tekkeh ;* and it is
usual for them to bring some small present every
time they visit him. As every detail of convent
life is symbolical, this custom is said to commemo-
rate the offerings brought by Gabriel to Adam, after
his expulsion from Paradise, and which, the legend
says, consisted of a kind of small loaves and corn,

with parrots and turtle doves for his entertainment, and swallows and hens for that of Eve.[1]

Each Order has its Chief Sheikh, or General, who resides in the city or town which contains the tomb of its founder (*Pir*), and is considered the guardian of the sacred relics. Bagdad, as mentioned in the preceding chapter, is the burial place of Abdul Kādr Ghilanī, the founder of the Kādiri Order, and his eminence in the Dervish world caused many succeeding *Pirs* to choose their place of sepulture in the neighbourhood of his tomb. This city is, consequently, a great centre of Dervish Generals. Konieh (Iconium), in Asia Minor, is the seat of the *Mevlevi* General, the successor and lineal descendant of the talented Jelālū-'d-Dīn. For the dignity of Sheikh is hereditary in the Mevlevi, Bektāshi, and Kādiri Orders. If the son be a minor at the death of his father, one of the elders is elected to act as his deputy (*Naib Khalifeh*) until he reaches the age of twenty. In the other Orders a council of Sheikhs, presided over by the General, choose a new Prior from among the disciples of the deceased *Murshid*, who do not appear to have any voice in the matter. Their choice falls, as a rule, on the elder who has so distinguished himself by his

[1] The Mohammedan legend says that the swallows were the means of reconciliation between Adam and Eve after their expulsion from Paradise when they had gone different ways. They found out Adam in Ceylon, and brought a hair of his beard to Eve who was at Jedda, returning with one of her hairs to Adam ; and the pair met on Mount Arafat, near Mekka.

spiritual advancement as to have previously held the post of Deputy Sheikh ; or, if such a functionary is not to be found in the convent, on one of the elders, generally the senior. The nomination is then notified to the Sheikh-ul-Islam, or Grand Mufti, from whose hands a new Prior must receive his investiture, even when he succeeds to the rule of a convent by right of heredity. This is, however, merely a matter of form, being a nominal acknow-ledgment of the Sheikh-ul-Islam as the spiritual head (under the Sultan) of the Mohammedan world ; for custom and prejudice have rendered it almost impossible for that dignitary to refuse to invest a Sheikh chosen by the Dervish primates. According to the rules of a few Orders, a Prior is free to leave his mantle of succession at his death to the disciple whom he may deem most worthy of it ; and in those Orders in which the office is hereditary in the family of its founder, if the Sheikh leave no son or immediate heir, the heads of several convents of the same Order meet and choose a successor ; or the members of his community elect one of their own number, generally the senior, to the vacant office. Such a choice is not, however, made without much deliberation, fasting, and prayer for divine guidance ; and, consequently, there is no unseemly rivalry among the brethren, for the result of their prayers and deliberations is looked upon as the revelation of the will of Allah, and their choice, made with such solemnity, is consequently ratified by the Grand Mufti without demur.

Many of the Dervish Sheikhs are *Seyyids*, or
lineal descendants of the family of the Prophet,
through the grandsons of his nephew and son-in-law,
the Khalif Ali, who escaped the massacre in which
their fathers, Hāsan and Husām—" The Martyrs "—
lost their lives.   *Seyyids* are distinguished by
their green turbans, and enjoy peculiar privi-
leges.   They are not under the same jurisdiction as
ordinary Mussulmans, but are ruled by a functionary called the *Nakeb-el-Eshref*, who resides
at Constantinople.   Everyone claiming to be a
descendant of the Prophet is required to possess a
document establishing his genealogy.

If a Sheikh is a celibate, he resides in the convent,
where a special apartment called the " cell of the
Master " is reserved for his use.   Many of the heads
of convents, however, are married, though it is
considered necessary for them to receive, in a vision,
a spiritual dispensation before taking to themselves
wives ; and such Priors appoint deputies to rule
over the monastic brethren in the convents during
their absence.   Like most Ottomans of the present
day they are, as a rule, monogamists, but not always,
nor are their wives always saintly women.
Some years ago I paid a visit to the harem of the
Mevlevi Prior of Magnesia (*ad Sipylum*), in
Asia Minor, who ranks next in the Order to the
General at Konieh.   He had two wives.   The *Bash
Kadin*, or first wife, to whom he had been married
some years, but who was childless, was dark-haired
and handsome, but with a rather haughty and

ill-tempered expression, increased, perhaps, by the
thick eyebrows painted to meet over the nose.
The second wife, not long a bride, was of the fair
Circassian type, brown-haired and blue-eyed, and
evidently a little in awe of her imperious-looking
companion. We were also courteously received
in the *selamlik* by the Sheikh, a handsome man in
the prime of life whose dignified presence was
enhanced by his flowing mantle of light fawn-
coloured cloth and his tall Dervish hat. One of
his neophytes, a fine youth of seventeen or there-
abouts, was, as we took our leave, commissioned by
his *Murshid* to show us some of the sights of the
town. Magnesia being built on the lower slopes
of Mount Sipylus, its upper streets are so steep that
they are terraced into staircases. As we toiled
upwards, the young Dervish, who was kindly carrying a little girl belonging to our party, was asked
by a group of children whom we passed, " Are you
not ashamed to be going about with Giaours ? "
The neophyte made no reply, but turned again with
an apologetic smile to continue his conversation
with the mother of the little girl. Had this mere
boy already learned the main precept of his Order,
which may be summed up in the one word—
LOVE ?

The domestic peace of another married Sheikh
at Adrianople was much disturbed by the unruly
temper of his wife. The garden of his house adjoined
that of an English lady, who, though she maintained friendly relations with the holy man, was

very often disturbed by the cries of his passionate
and ill-tempered spouse. Nor could the good
man make use of his privilege of divorce to rid
himself of his uncongenial helpmeet, as he was
not in a position to pay the sum promised in the
marriage contract (*nekyah*) in case of such a
contingency.

Early one morning my friend was disturbed by
cries of " Fire " (*Yangen var !*) proceeding from the
Sheikh's abode. Snatching up a can of water, she
hastened downstairs, and, followed by her servants
with pails, entered her neighbour's premises through
a gate in the garden wall. No indications of a
conflagration were, however, visible. But in front
of the house stood the Dervish with his ebony arm-
rest in his hand, while on the ground sat his wife,
sobbing hysterically ; and it was only too evident
that the holy man's patience had been at last tried
beyond further endurance, and that he had
administered the correction that had been only too
long deserved.

To arrive at the degree of spirituality required
in those who fill the office of Deputy Prior, a
Dervish must have spent much time in prayer,
fasting, and complete abstraction from all worldly
pursuits. Besides being far advanced on the
spiritual path, and familiar with all the mystical
dogmas and tenets of the Order, he must possess
the respect, reverence, and entire submission of the
rest of the community. By constant prayer and the
continued performance of the *Zikr*, his breath, and

even his touch, should have acquired a sanctifying and healing influence, and he must also be believed to possess the power of working miracles. He will be favoured with visions, and by their import his superior is able to judge when his spiritual training may be considered complete, when he terminates the period of his seclusion. He will then commence his pilgrimage to the holy cities and the tombs of the saints, and, perhaps, may proceed as far as Bagdad, if the founder of his Order be among the many saints buried there, when it will also be his duty to visit the burial place of the grandsons of the Prophet at Kerbeleh, in the vicinity of that city.

Each of the twelve members of a Bektāshi fraternity has some special office attached to his *postaki* (sheepskin seat). Some of these would appear to entail a certain amount of manual labour, while others have merely nominal, or at most only occasional, duties. They are as follows :—

1. The Sheikh.
2. The Cook.
3. The Baker.
4. The Deputy Shekh.
5. The Superintendent.
6. The Steward.
7. The Coffee-maker.
8. The Bagbearer.
9. The Sacrificer.
10. The attendant of the *Tekkeh*.
11. The Groom.[1]
12. The attendant on the guests.

[1] Commemorative of Kamber, the groom of the Khalif Ali.

The other Orders appear to have officers more or less similar to these attached to the service of the convent.

Though all Dervishes are free to leave the Order into which they have originally entered and join another, or even to return to the world, it is very rare that any use is made of the liberty. Each member seems to regard it as a sacred duty to remain faithful for life to the Order that first received him, and in its dress to end his days. To this spirit of devotion they add that of perfect submission to the will of their Prior. " Consider your guide (*Murshid*) as the greatest of all guides," and " Whatever you do or think, let your Sheikh be always present to your mind," are two primary obligations expressed by a formula called the *rabouta*, which is repeated by them as scrupulously as is the *namāz* by the orthodox Mohammedans. Humility of spirit and demeanour are required from all ; they are taught not to consider themselves superior to others, but to rank themselves as the poorest, lowest, and most humble of mankind. Hence, not only in the cloister, but in all their dealings with the outer world, these mystics are distinguished by the deep humility of their manner. Their heads are ever bent, their gaze absorbed ; and the words *Ay b' Allah* (Thanks to God) are ever upon their lips. They must not divulge the secrets of the Order to their wives or relatives, nor to anyone who is not, like them, a " seeker after the Truth."

Special forms of salutation are used by the

Dervishes. As the *Love of God* is the principal of the Mevlevis, their salutation is " Let it be Love ! " (*Eshk olsoun*) ; but that in general use among the Orders is " *Ya Hoo !* " (O Him). After the reception of a Dervish into an Order the only salutation required of him on entering the *Tekkeh* is to incline his head gently towards the Sheikh, and lay the right hand across the breast near the neck, in token of perfect submission to him. It is said that brethren not in costume recognise each other in public by placing the right hand, as if accidentally, on the chin. It is also customary for Dervishes when entering the *Tekkeh* or on meeting each other, to place the right hand on the heart, and, gently inclining the body, to exclaim " *Yā Hoo, Erens!* " (O Him, Brethren), the reply to which is "*Ay Vallah, Shahim* (Good, by Allah, my Shah). On making an enquiry concerning the health, they say, " Health, my Joys ! " and the reply is " Good, by Allah, my brother." Their other salutations on meeting and taking leave are *Hoo, dost Erenler* (Him, dear friend), and *Aye Vallah Hoo dost*. Towards those who are not Dervishes they, however, use the ordinary beautiful Mohammedan greeting, *Salaam aleikoum* (Peace be to thee).

There are special prayers and formulas for every event and detail of convent life. Those of the Bektāshis are seventy-six in number, and are called by the symbolical name of " *Interpreters*." On crossing the doorsill of the *Tekkeh*, they say :—

" I have placed my head and my heart on the

sill of the door of repentance, so that my body may
be pure as gold.   Deign, O Sheikh, to turn your
eyes for an instant on this poor man (*faqir*)."

On presenting an offering to his superior, the
disciple says :—

" The ant brought as an offering to Solomon the
thigh of a grasshopper.   Thou, O Sheikh, art
Solomon, and I am thy ant ; accept my humble
offering."

On asking for hospitality at a *Tekkeh*, or *Turbéh*,
the traveller says :—

" Allah is our Friend !   Peace to the dwellers in
this *Tekkeh*.   Love to those who are joyful, and to
all the poor men (*fouqara*) now present ; to the *Pirs*
and to the Sheikhs ; to the dwellers in this house of
the Shāh (Ali)."

The grace before meals of the Bektāshis differs
from that used by the Kādiris and the generality of
the Orders.   It runs thus :—

" O Allah !   O Allah !   By the horn of the arch-
angel Isrâfeel !   by the symbolism of Kamber !   by
the light of the Prophet !   by the altar and the pulpit !
by our sovereign *Pir*, Hadji Bektāsh Vali !   by our
General !   by the breath (*nefs*) of the Three, the Five,
the Seven, and the Forty True Saints, we thank
Thee.   *Hoo !* "

The following is the grace used by the Kādiris.
That of the other Orders differs from it only in the
name of the founder :—

" Praise be to Allah !   May He increase His
bounties.   By the blessings of Abraham !   By the

Light of the Prophet ! By the grace of Ali ! By the war cry of Mohammed ! By the secret of Abdul Kādr Ghilāni, we beseech Thee to be gracious to our Lord (the *Pir*)." It is a rule of the Order of the Hamzavīs, obligatory on all members, to retain in their minds during their meals, both when with others as well as when alone, a continual remembrance of God ; and after they have eaten, to offer devout thanks.

Notwithstanding that all the Orders are nominally mendicant, and dependent for subsistence on the offerings of the pious, begging is strictly forbidden, save among the Bektāshis and wandering Dervishes. These, who deem it meritorious to live upon alms, frequent the bazaars and public streets for the purpose of recommending themselves to the charity of passers-by. Their formula of request is generally " Something, for the love of Allah." Many Bektāshis, however, make it a rule to support themselves by handicraft trades, and particularly by making, in imitation of their *Pir*, Hadji Bektāsh, small articles of wood, such as spoons, ladles, bowls, and graters. They also carve out of pieces of marble the fastenings used by Dervishes of that order for their belts and for the collars of their garments, and fashion the two-beaked bowls (*keshgool*) used by the mendicants when soliciting alms. The monastic brethren belonging to the other and endowed Orders are supplied only with food and lodging at the expense of the *Tekkeh*. Their meals, which are very simple, and consist, as a rule, of two dishes only, are usually eaten in the solitude of the cells ; but on certain occasions the brethren dine together in the common room. Each Dervish is required to provide himself with dress and other necessaries, and, though living in the convent, follows some trade or profession. Those who are good calligraphists find employment in copying the Koran and other religious books. If any are without resources, they seldom fail to receive contributions either from their relations, an allowance from the Prior, or a pension from some wealthy individual. For although, as above remarked, the members of the majority of the Order are forbidden to *ask* for alms, they are allowed to accept gifts when offered by charitable persons " for the love of Allah." The rule against begging appears also to be relaxed in the case of Dervishes on their pilgrimage, as they are then usually without their ordinary means of support. Many Mohammedans reserve their alms exclusively for the Dervishes, and make it their duty to seek out those of high reputation for sanctity, visit them frequently, and supply their wants. Others, again, even lodge and board holy men in their houses, in the hope of thus drawing upon themselves, their families, and their fortunes the blessings of heaven.

All married Dervishes reside with their families, but sleep in the convent once or twice a week on the nights preceding their religious exercises. No married Dervish is, however, allowed to pass the night in the *Tekkeh* of the Mevlevi General at Konieh. The lay brethren, after passing their novitiate in the *Tekkeh*, return to their ordinary avocations ; withdrawing, however, as much as possible from all intercourse with the world, and endeavouring to lead spiritual and holy lives.

Various forms of punishment and penance are imposed on erring Dervishes by their Sheikh according to the gravity of the offence. Evliya Effendi says that when a disciple has committed any fault or breach of discipline, he is judged by a council composed of the Prior and the elders, and sentenced to a term of imprisonment not exceeding three days, as a longer period of incarceration might be detrimental to his family and worldly affairs. The council are, however, careful to examine well into any accusation, and not to punish the defaulter too severely. In former times the bastinado was inflicted by the Sheikh on his erring disciples. He was, however, required, when striking, never to lift the stick higher than his ear, to do which was reckoned " mere injustice and passionate behaviour." Another punishment was that of carrying a heavy stone suspended round the neck, a custom which is said to have originated with Moses. [1] It is a sin for a Dervish to speak a word which is contrary to the four " gates," or principles of Justice, Truth, Order, and Knowledge. One who speaks useless or purposeless words is said to have strayed from the Path (*Tariq*). This general habit of reticence is variously illustrated in Dervish writings. " A Dervish, when asked by one of his brethren what

[1] See p. 115.

marvellous gift he had brought back with him
from the garden of delights he had visited in his
ecstatic trance, replied : ' I intended, on arriving
at the Rosebush (the presence of Allah) to fill the
skirt of my robe with roses, in order to offer them
to my brethren on my return. But when I arrived
at the Rosebush, its odour so intoxicated my senses
that the hem of my robe escaped from my grasp.'
Silent is the tongue of the man who has known Allah." [1]

It is also related of Jelālū-'d-Dīn that when one
day on a visit to a fellow Sheikh of great repute, he
was asked by a Dervish who happened to be present,
" What is Poverty ? " Jelāl returned no answer,
and the question was thrice repeated. When the
poet left, the Sheikh, after accompanying him to
the door, returned to the Dervish and severely
reprimanded him for his insolent intrusion on his
distinguished guest, which, he said, " was the more
inexcusable as he (Jelāl) fully answered thy question
the first time thou didst put it." The Dervish,
surprised, asked what the answer had been. " A
poor man (*faqir*)," replied the Prior, " is one who,
having known Allah, hath his tongue tied." [2]

Many Dervishes voluntarily practise a most rigid
abstinence. Those of the Khalvetī Order occasionally perform a painful fast of forty days' duration,
living during that period on bread and water alone.
As mentioned in a preceding chapter, the word
Khalvet signifies " retirement," and the Sheikh of
that name who founded this Order practised it to

[1] The *Mesnevi*.   [2] *Ibid.*

a great extent.[1] Devout Dervishes in all the
Orders condemn themselves to the performance of
acts of the utmost austerity, and remain for a long
time shut up in their cells for the purposes of prayer
and meditation. Certain nights being considered
peculiarly holy as anniversaries of some event
in the life of the Prophet,[2] these are specially
consecrated to penitence and prayer. In order to
drive away sleep, some will stand for whole nights
in constrained attitudes; others, in order to maintain
themselves in a sitting posture, tie their hair to a
cord hanging from the ceiling, a practice called
chilleh ; others again fasten their limbs together
with a leather strap passed round their necks and
holding the knees up to the chin.

If a Dervish, when on his pilgrimage to the holy
places, neglects or fails to perform any of the prescribed rites and ceremonies attached to that
sacred duty, he atones for it by a sacrifice. On the
same principle, a Dervish who finds himself guilty
under other circumstances of a sin of omission or
commission, brands himself with a hot iron in order
to avoid the punishment of purgatorial fires in the
next world. According to Evliya Effendi, " those

[1] See above, p. 18.
[2] For instance, the anniversary of the Prophet's birth ;
the 27th night of Ramazan, called the " Night of Power,"
at one moment of which, according to popular belief, all
inanimate things—trees, plants and mountains—bow themselves in adoration of Allah, and all waters taste sweet ;
and the " Excellent Night," the 10th of the month of
Shaban when the Recording Angels deliver up their books
to the Almighty, and commence new ones.

who have a hundred and one scars on their heads proclaim that they have tried a hundred and one spiritual paths, and have abandoned everything connected with the world ; those who wear on their foreheads the ' scar of resignation ' signify by it that they cherish in their hearts no desire but Allah ; those who brand their ears, that they have renounced their own wills and live only to fulfil that of Allah."

Every convent, and every shrine at which a Dervish resides, has one or more guest-chambers which are at the disposal of travelling Dervishes of any Order, and in which, especially if no other place of refuge is at hand, other Mussulmans on their pilgrimage are made welcome. It is the special duty of one of the brethren to attend upon the guests, bring them food from the common kitchen, and perform the other little rites of Oriental hospitality, such as making their coffee and preparing their chibouks for smoking. If the guest be a Sheikh, he is received in the apartment of the Superior of the convent, and otherwise treated with special consideration.

The funeral of a Dervish Sheikh of high repute is a most impressive and interesting ceremony. Besides his own congregation, the members of other Orders in the neighbourhood, together with a large concourse of the male population, assemble at the *Tekkeh* to follow the departed to his last resting-place. After the usual burial service, called the *mihit namāz*, has been performed in the monastery,

four or more of the disciples of the deceased Sheikh
take up on their shoulders the rude coffin, which is
covered with shawls, and bears at the head his turban.
The bereaved fraternity proceed slowly towards the
cemetery, uttering at intervals the exclamation,
" Allah ! Allah ! " Behind follows the long and
irregular procession, winding along the narrow
streets. In the Turkish quarter the women peep
through their latticed blinds with reverent curiosity,
and in the Christian *mahallahs* lean out of their
open windows to watch its progress. There are
Mevlevi Dervishes in tall hats and flowing mantles ;
Bektāshis in close round caps and black robes ;
orthodox Imāms in their ample white turbans ; and
townspeople of every creed in multicoloured garments, with here and there a soldier or official in
tasselled fez, all pacing with bowed heads and
sedate looks. If a mosque or *Tekkeh* is passed
on the route, the coffin is deposited in front of the
gateway and a service chanted, the whole assembly
solemnly joining in the refrain of *Amin ! Amin !*
A fresh relay of bearers then raises the coffin, and
the solemn procession moves on.

CHAPTER VI

THE STAGES OF INITIATION

" And he who hopes to scale the heights
  Without enduring pain,
And toil, and strife, but wastes his life
  In idle quest and vain."

THE founder of one of the earliest Orders of
Dervishes, Sheikh Olwān, laid down certain rules to
be observed in the admission of new members into
his Brotherhood ; and these rules, though subsequently elaborated by certain of the Orders, are
still substantially the same in their leading features,
differing only in the severity of the discipline
imposed upon a candidate, in the length of his
period of probation, and in certain minor details.

As a general rule, a neophyte is required during his
novitiate to live in complete retirement from the
world, to perform the menial offices of the *Tekkeh*,
and to repeat daily 101, 151, or 301 times one of
the attributes of the Deity.   These are ninety-seven
in number, and are called the *Isāmi Ilahi*, or "Beautiful Names of Allah."   Seven only of these are used
by a *Murid ;* they are *La ilaha il Allah* (" There is
no God but Allah ") ; *Yā Allah* (" O God ") ; *Yā
Hoo* (" O Him ") ; *Yā Hakk* (" O Truth ") ; *Yā
Hay* (" O Ever Living ") ; *Yā Kayyoum* (" O Self-
existent ") ;   and *Yā Kahhar* (" O Almighty ").
In the first stage of his probation the neophyte
repeats only the first attribute, and his advancement

through the seven successive stages depends upon the proofs he is able to give of the reality of his vocation for a Dervish life. These proofs are found in the frequency and vividness of the dreams and visions vouchsafed to him, which he is bound to communicate to his Superior.

Admission into the Mevlevi Order is only obtained by the performance of an uninterrupted novitiate of a thousand and one consecutive days. Should the *Murid* fail in a single day's duties, or be absent from the *Tekkeh* for one whole night, his probation must be re-commenced; and, whatever his worldly rank, he must consider himself the subordinate of every member of the *Tekkeh*. He is instructed in his duties by the *Ashjibashi*, or Chief of the Kitchen, spends much of his time in prayer and fasting, and in committing to memory the prayers and passages of the Koran more especially used by his Order. He must also become proficient in the mystic dance, and take part in the public services of the Brotherhood. The novice, having passed through his period of probation to the satisfaction of the Chief of the Kitchen, that functionary—who acts as his sponsor—reports him to the Sheikh as worthy of admission to the initiatory grade of the Order, and a meeting of all the Brotherhood is convened in the *Ismi Jelih Hujreh*, the private assembly room of the *Tekkeh*. When all are assembled, the *Murid* is led by the *Ashjibashi* to the Prior, who occupies the seat of honour in the angle of the divan; he kisses the extended hand of his Superior, and seats himself on the floor before him. His sponsor then places his right hand on the neck, and his left on the forehead of the neophyte, the Sheikh takes off the *kulah* which, with the rest of the Mevlevi costume he has worn during his novitiate, and proceeds to chant a Persian distich composed by the founder of the Order. He then delivers an exhortation to the young disciple, at the termination of which he replaces the *kulah* on his head. The *Murid* and his sponsor now place themselves in the middle of the room, where they assume a posture of profound humility, standing with folded arms, crossed toes, and bowed heads. The *Ashjibashi* is then addressed as follows by the Sheikh :—

" May the services of the *Murid*, thy brother, be agreeable to the Throne of the Eternal, and in the eyes of our *Pir ;* may His satisfaction, His felicity, and His glory grow in the nest of the humble, in the cell of the poor. Let us exclaim *Hoo* (Him) in honour of our *Mevlana.*" [1] The *Murid* and his sponsor answer " *Hoo !* " and the former then kisses the hand of the Sheikh, who addresses to him some paternal remarks on his new position, and concludes by asking all the members of the congregation to embrace and welcome their new brother.

A novice of the Bektāshi Order is also required to perform a novitiate of a thousand and one days, during which he frequents the services of the *Tekkeh*. But the formalities observed by this Order in the reception of candidates differ from those of

[1] The founder of the Order, *Mevlana* Jelālū-'d-Dīn.

the Mevlevi Brethren, and are even more elaborate.
A candidate is recommended to the Sheikh by two
members of the community who are called his " Interpreters." [1] He must also have already given during
his novitiate proofs of spiritual knowledge and
acquirements, and have faithfully kept certain
pretended secrets of the Order imparted to him as
tests of his powers of reticence. His reception into
the Brotherhood is also determined by the revelations concerning him received, in dreams or visions,
by the Sheikh from the *Pir* or from Ali. What
is thus revealed is not communicated to the
neophyte.

On the evening appointed for the ceremony of
initiation—for the services of the Bektāshi Order
are always held by night—the neophyte takes with
him to the convent a sheep and a small sum of
money. The sheep is sacrificed on the threshold of
the *Tekkeh*, part of its wool is twisted into a rope,
the rest being preserved to be made later on into a
girdle for his use. If the candidate desires to take
the vow of celibacy, he is stripped naked ; but if
he proposes, as in the generality of cases, to take
only the ordinary, or secular vow of this widespread and numerous Order, his breast only is
bared. With the rope round his neck he is led by
his " Interpreters," one of whom carries the symbol
termed the *tebber*, a kind of battle-axe, into the hall
of the *Tekkeh*. Here he stands with his arms folded

[1] *Terjumān.* This term also signifies the secret pass-
word or phrase of the Bektāshi Order.

across his breast, his hands on his shoulders, his toes crossed, and his body inclined towards the Sheikh — a posture signifying abject humility and designated *buyun kesmék*. The Prior and the Twelve Elders are seated around the hall on their sheepskins, a lighted candle being placed in front of each. One of the " Interpreters " announces to the Prior that he has brought to him a slave, and requests his acceptance of the gift. He acquiesces, and the neophyte, addressing him, repeats this prayer :—

" I have erred ; pardon my fault, O Shah ! For the sake of the Accepted One (Ali) of the Exalted Place ; for the sake of the Martyr (Hussein). I have done wrong to myself, and to our Lord, and I implore pardon of Him."

His " fault " is supposed to consist in having so long delayed to join the Order. The Sheikh then recites a sort of Litany, to which the *Murid* makes the responses.

" In the Name of Allah, the Merciful and the Clement :—

" I beseech Allah's forgiveness (thrice repeated) ; I have come to implore pardon ; I have come in search of the Truth ; I ask it for the sake· of the Just. Truth is the path which leads to Allah, the All True, whom I know. What you term Evil, I also know to be Evil, and I will avoid taking with my hands what is another's. . . . Repent of your sins unto Allah, a repentance that knows not return unto sin."

Then follows an exhortation by the Superior :—

"Eat nothing forbidden ; speak no falsehood ; quarrel with none ; be kind to your inferiors ; overlook the faults of others, and conceal them. If you cannot do this with your hand, do it with your skirts, your tongue, and your heart."

The novice then kisses the hand of the Sheikh, who continues :—

"If thou now accept me as thy father, I accept thee as my son. Be hereafter the pledge of Allah breathed in thy right ear."

He then repeats after his Superior the words : "Mohammed is my leader, and Ali is my guide." The Sheikh asks, "Dost thou accept me as thy Guide (meaning as the representative of Ali) ? " to which he responds, "I accept thee as my Guide " ; and the Sheikh adds, "Then I accept thee as my son."

The postulant is now led by his " Interpreters " to the Sheikh, before whom he first bows low and then prostrates himself, touching the floor with his forehead. Kneeling opposite to him so closely that their knees touch, the Superior takes the postulant's right hand in his, and the thumbs are raised to represent the Arabic letter *Alif*. The latter places his ear to the mouth of the Sheikh who imparts to him in a whisper the *Ikrānāmeh*, or secret Vows of the Order. As the tenets of the Bektāshis are believed by many to be purely pantheistic, it is asserted that the words whispered by the Sheikh to the *Murid* convey a doctrine to which he must assent on pain of death, and admit the unity of God and Nature. But this assertion is positively denied by others ; and it would, indeed, be difficult to prove it, as the secrets of the Order are never committed to writing, and are known only to its members, who, it is believed, are deterred by the most frightful penalties from divulging them.

When the disciple is presented with the girdle and the stone worn in it, the Prior, as he binds it round his waist says to him : " I now bind up thy waist in the path of Allah—O Holy Name, possessed of all knowledge ! Whoever knows this Name will become the successor of his Sheikh (*Naib*)." Certain principles of the Order are then imparted to the novice, who is also instructed in various mystic tenets concerning the universe and the Koran. The Sheikh then sums up by saying, " There is but one Light, and the Truth is (as) the Moon. He who has found the science of his own body (called the *Ilum i Vurgood*, his spiritual counterpart [1]) knows his Lord ; for the holy Prophet has said, ' To know thyself is to know thy Lord.' In this is comprised a knowledge of thine own secret, and that of thy Creator."

When a Bektāshi takes the vow of celibacy, he is asked by the Sheikh whether, if he break it, he is willing to come under the sword of Ali, to which he replies in the affirmative. The inner signification of this phrase is said to contain one of the secret

[1] See above, p. 36.

vows of the Order. On putting on for the first time the sash or *Alif-lam*,[1] he says, " I abandon all matrimony, and bind myself by this sash so to do." The *Murid* then recites chapter cxii of the Koran ; after which the Sheikh declares to him that " Allah doth not engender or bring forth, and so may men tell of thee, and no one is equal to Him."

Twelve being the Bektāshi mystical number, a member having broken a vow, incurs twelve punishments. One of their secret signs is said to consist of the words *Tebran* and *Toolan*—" far " and " near " —signifying " near in affection and far in conceit."

The ceremonies of affiliation of the other Orders bear a great resemblance to the foregoing, with the exception of those of the *Kādiri*, the *Rūfa'i*, the *Sā'di*.

A novice of the *Rūfa'i* receives from the Sheikh a small cup of water from the *Zemzem*—the Sacred Well of Mekka—which, after reciting a prayer over, he drinks.

At the initiation of a *Sādi* Dervish, a number of dates are placed before the Superior. He selects one, extracts the stone, breathes upon the fruit and puts it into the mouth of the neophyte who is seated on the floor before him. Two members of the Order seat themselves to the right and left of him, and proceed to sway him from side to side, reciting at the same time: " There is no God but Allah," the Sheikh doing the same, until he has swallowed the date. All then rise, and the *Murid*, after kissing

---

[1] The first and last letters of the Arabic alphabet.

the hand of the superior, is acknowledged as a brother by the rest of the congregation.

A person wishing to join the *Kādiri* Order intimates his desire to one of its members. The Dervish enjoins him to frequent the *Tekkeh* and its services, and also to wait upon the brethren and their guests. These menial duties are required from every neophyte, whatever his worldly rank may be. The period of probation lasts for many months, during which time the *Murid* becomes greatly attached to his Superior. When he has been deemed worthy to enter the ranks of the Dervishes, he is directed to procure a cap of plain white felt, which is carried by his sponsor to the Sheikh. A *gul*, or piece of cloth stamped into the shape of a rose of eighteen petals, and having in the centre the " Solomon's Seal "—two interlaced triangles—is then attached to it. When the brethren assemble in the *Tekkeh* for the performance of the *Zikr*, or invocation of Allah, the Sheikh takes his place on his sheepskin and the neophyte, led by his sponsor, kneels before him and kisses his hand. The Sheikh takes off the novice's ordinary cap, and replaces it by that bearing the " Rose," which he has carried in his bosom, and says, three times, " *Allahu Ekber* " (God is Great).

A disciple does not, however, even after this formal reception into it, become at once a full member of the Order. This grade is only reached after, it may be, years of further probation, and its attainment depends upon the proofs he is able to

give of his progress in spirituality. His final
admission to full brotherhood is usually determined
by a revelation from the *Pir*, or from Ali, received
simultaneously by himself and his Sheikh. While
passing through these intermediate stages, the
aspirant is under the guidance of the Superior or of
an initiate who has himself reached the highest
degree. During the first stage, which is termed
Sheriãt, or " the Law," the disciple observes all the
usual rites of Moslem worship, obeys all the commands and precepts of the Koran like any other
True Believer, and is treated by the Brethren of
the community as an uninitiated outsider. He is
taught at the same time to concentrate his thoughts
so completely on his " Guide " as to become mentally
absorbed in him as a spiritual link with the supreme
object of all devotion. This Guide must be the
neophyte's shield against all worldly thoughts and
desires ; his spirit must aid him in all his efforts,
accompany him wherever he may be, and be ever
present to his mental vision. Such a frame of mind
is termed "annihilation into the *Murshid*," and
the Guide discovers, by means of his own visions,
the degree of spirituality to which his disciple has
attained, and to what extent his soul has become
absorbed into his own.

The *Murid* now enters upon what, in Dervish
phraseology, is called " the Path." During this
period, which forms in reality the transition from
outward to hidden things, the disciple is familiar-
ised with those philosophical writings of the great

Sūfi masters which form the chief subject of the
lectures and studies of the Order. He is taught to
substitute spiritual for ritual worship, and led by
degrees to abandon the dogmas and formulas of
Islam as necessary only for the unenlightened
masses. This method is, however, pursued with
great tact and caution, for a disciple is not released
from the usual observances of religion until he has
given proof of sincere piety, virtue, exceptional
spirituality, and extreme asceticism ; and a Dervish
at this stage of his novitiate passes most of his time
in solitary contemplation, endeavouring to detach
his mind from all visible objects in order to attain
the desired union with the Deity.   His Guide, meanwhile, imparts to him his own mystical philosophy
as he finds him capable of receiving it. If the
disciple's religious feelings appear to be shocked by
any maxim to which he has given utterance, the
already mentioned Jesuitical expedient known as the
Ketman supplies the Master with a double sense which
enables him at once to convince his disciple of the
groundlessness of his objections.   If, on the contrary,
the *Murshid* finds his pupil's theological digestion
robust, his advance on the path will be correspond-
ingly rapid.   He is now supposed to come under the
spiritual influence of the *Pir*, or founder of the Order,
in whom he in turn becomes mentally absorbed to
such a degree as to be virtually one with him,
acquiring his attributes and power of performing
supernatural acts.

The next stage of the mystic life is that termed

by the Dervishes " Spiritual Knowledge," and the disciple who believes himself, and is believed by his Sheikh to have attained to such knowledge or, in other words, to have become inspired, is held to be on an equality with the Angels. He now enters into spiritual communion with the Prophet himself, into whose soul his own has become absorbed.

The fourth degree is usually attained during the forty days of fasting and seclusion, observed by every Dervish during his novitiate. In his ecstatic state he believes himself to have become a part of the Divinity, and sees Him in all things. The Sheikh, after witnessing this remarkable proof of the success of his teachings, gently awakens the disciple from his ecstasy, and having restored him to his normal condition, bestows upon him the rank of *khalifeh* (" successor "). The mystic now resumes his outward observance of the rites of Islam, and prepares for his pilgrimage to the Holy Cities.

Not every Dervish, however, attains even to the third grade ; and the highest is attained only by the few. Those less spiritually gifted, or less mystically minded, still continue to recognise the personal and anthropomorphic Allah of the Koran, and look forward at death only to a closer intimacy with Him than that which will be enjoyed by those who have not entered on " the Path."

CHAPTER VII

THE COSTUMES, MUSICAL INSTRUMENTS, AND SYMBOLIC OBJECTS OF THE DERVISHES

" . . . . . flutes
In Dervish hands at mystic dance,
Whose hopes or fears, loves, joys, or cares,
Are whispered in ecstatic trance."
IZZET MOLLA, *The Reedpen's Reply*.

" Stone about its waist begirdled, and with iron
staff in hand,
Tremblingly the compass-needle seeketh for the
Loved One's Land."
JĀMĪ.

THE Dervishes of the various Orders may be easily distinguished from their fellow-men, and also, generally, from each other, by their costumes, and, more particularly, by the shape of their head-dresses; and to the latter, as well as to every other article of their clothing, some symbolic meaning, and, in many cases, some legend is attached.

The out-of-door costume of the Mevlevi Order is said to have been adopted by their talented founder Mevlāna (Our Lord) Jelālū-'d-Dīn, as a sign of mourning for his friend and spiritual master, Shemsū-'d-Dīn ("Sun of the Faith"). It consists of a tall hat called a *kulah*, of undyed camel's hair felt, in shape like an inverted plantpot. Their Sheikhs, who all claim descent from the family of the Prophet, are, on this account, entitled to wear round their *kulah* a green turban. The legend attached to this head-dress says that the soul of Mohammed had a previous existence in the *Alemi Ervah*, or Spirit World, where Allah placed it in a vase of light of that shape. The lay members of the Order, who do not wear the Dervish dress except when taking part in its ceremonies, often, when in private, lay aside their ordinary fez, or turban, and don the *kulah*, in order to enjoy the happy influence it is believed to exert on the wearer. When the son of Othman I, Solyman Pasha, asked the blessing of the Mevlevi Grand Master at Konieh on the expedition he was undertaking against the Byzantine Greeks, that dignitary placed on his head a *kulah*, and prophesied that " victory should go with him." The prince showed his reverence for the gift by having it covered with silver. So high was the favour which this Order enjoyed under the early Sultans, that their *kulah* became the state head-dress at the Ottoman Court. It was worn, ornamented with gold embroidery, by successive " Commanders of the Faithful," and also, variously decorated, by civil and military dignitaries until the beginning of the present century, when " the Reforming Sultan," Mahmoud II, relegated its use to the officers of the Janissary Corps.

The *khirkha* of the Mevlevi Order is a long, loose, wide-sleeved robe of fawn-coloured cloth for ordinary wear, and of black stuff when used to cover the costume in which they dance. Like the mantles of the Dervishes generally, it is more or less a copy of that believed to have been worn by the Prophet.

The *tennūri*, or skirt, is worn only by Mevlevi Dervishes when performing their religious exercises. It may be red, yellow, or brown ; is made very wide and without gores, and reaches to the feet. The rapid motion of the wearers when spinning round in their mystic dance extends these skirts to their full width, exposing to view the drawers of white linen worn beneath. The upper part of the body is clad in a short jacket of coloured material with tight-fitting sleeves, and round the waist is bound the *taybend*, a girdle containing in its folds the " Stone of Contentment." This is commemorative of the stones formerly carried by begging Dervishes, who bound them close to their stomachs in order to suppress the pangs of hunger. Three were usually carried, though their wearers confidently believed that Allah would not fail to send relief before the necessity arose for using the full number.

The use of vocal and instrumental music by this Order is said to have been adopted by its founder in order to rouse the lethargic natures of the inhabitants of Rūm to a devotional love of Allah through the allurement of sweet sounds addressed to their outward senses. The orchestra of their chief *Tekkeh* at Konieh is composed of six different instruments, among which are the reedflute and zither, the rebeck, a kind of violoncello, drums, and tambourines. In the generality of their *Tekkehs*, however, only zithers, reedflutes, and small hemispherical drums are used. The music of these flutes appears to have a singularly entrancing effect on the Dervishes whose exercises it accompanies. They are lulled and soothed by it to a forgetfulness of the visible world as if they indeed heard in its strains the mystic voices of the spiritual world. In the " Song of the Reed-flute " above quoted,[1] the Dervish poet symbolises under the figure of a Lover sighing for his absent Mistress, the Soul of Man languishing for reunion with the Divine Love. In the *Mesnevi* of Jelālū-'d-Dīn is given the following charmingly poetical account of the origin of the reed-flute's mystic music which recalls the beautiful myth of Orpheus and his lute.

" One day the Prophet privately imparted to Ali the Secrets and Mysteries of the ' Brethren of Sincerity '—evidently the original Brotherhood—with the injunction not to reveal them to anyone. For forty days Ali kept these secrets locked in his breast, but feeling no longer able to contain them, he fled into the desert. Coming upon a well, he stooped as far as possible down its mouth, and to the earth and water divulged, one by one, these mysteries. Some days afterwards a shepherd youth, whose heart had been miraculously enlightened, perceived a single reed growing up out of the well. He cut it down, drilled holes in it, and, while pasturing his sheep in the neighbourhood, breathed through the flute he had made melodies like those performed by the Dervish Lovers of Allah. Soon the various Arab tribes heard of the youth's wonderful flute-playing, and came to listen to it, accompanied

[1] See p. 52.

by their sheep and camels, which forgot to graze while hearkening. The nomad shepherds wept for joy and delight, and broke forth into transports and ecstasies. The fame of this music at length reached the Prophet, who sent for the youthful musician. When he began to play before them, all the holy disciples of Allah's Messenger were moved to tears ; they burst forth into shouts and exclamations of pure bliss, and lost all earthly consciousness. When he had ceased, the Prophet declared that the notes of the shepherd's pipe were the interpretation of the Holy Mysteries which he had confided to the keeping of Ali.

" Thus it is," adds the author, " that, until a man acquires the sincere devotion of the linnet-voiced reedflute, he cannot hear in its dulcet tones the Mysteries of the Brethren of Sincerity, nor realise the delights thereof ; for faith is altogether a yearning of the heart and a gratification of the spiritual sense.

"The pangs my love for thee excites, can I to mortal breathe?
Ah no l Like Ali's, some pure fount my sighs, too, must receive.
Perchance some reeds may thence upspring its brink to overgrow,
And plaintive flutes those reeds become to murmur forth my woe."

The cap, mantle, and girdle of the Bektāshi Order are called by their wearers " The Three Principles," or " Points," and have the following legendary origin. The Angel Gabriel on the occasion of one of his visits to the Prophet, cut his hair, shaved his beard, and then invested him with a cap, mantle, and girdle. This act of service the Angel had previously performed only for Adam and Abraham. Mohammed then proceeded to do for Ali what Gabriel had done for him, and Ali in his turn performed this office for the Twelve Imāms.

Much symbolic significance is also attached to the Bektāshi cap. It is called a *Taj*, or "crown," and is of white felt, shaped like a dome, and divided into four parts by grooves, called "Doors," which allude to the four great stages of the spiritual life. These "Doors" are subdivided by other three grooves into twelve parts, in remembrance of the twelve Imāms, and signify also the abandonment of twelve sins. The green or black turban worn round the cap is called the "parable" (*Istīva*). It signifies the abandonment of the world for the pursuit of high and holy things. As a general rule, the Sheikhs alone wear turbans. They, however, frequently appoint deputies who, as they bear the same honorary title, are also entitled to wear this distinctive head-dress. The cap has, besides, thirteen mystical significations attached to its several parts, among which are its border, circumference, "key," or apex, and decoration. This cap is, spiritually speaking, of two kinds : the "Crown of the Ignorant" (*Tāj i Jahil*), the wearers of which are often to be seen in the bazaars and public streets ; and the "Crown of the Perfect" (*Tāj i Kiamil*), worn by those who shun, rather than seek, intercourse with the world.

There are also other forms of the Bektāshi *Tāj*, for, according to their saying : " As all the letters of the alphabet grew out of the first one, *Alif*, so the caps of the various Orders were derived from the *Alifer*, or original cap." It is sometimes also called " the Founder " (*Pir*), and was in earlier times inscribed with the text : " All things will perish, save His face, and to Him will all things return." On putting it on, the Dervish recites this invocation :—

" Sign of the glorious [name of the *Pir* of his Order]; of Kamber, [the groom of Ali]; of those who are dead ; of the great family of the Imām Riza ; [1] permit me to put on this Crown, for I fully believe in its virtues. Great is Allah."

The mantle of the Bektāshi Order, though similar in shape, differs from that of the Mevlevi Dervishes in being decorated with twelve lines, or stripes, symbolical, like the grooves in their " Crowns," of the Twelve Imāms, and is edged with green. Among its mystical attributes are the following, with their meanings as given by the fourth Imām, *Jafer-es-Sadik*.

Its " True Faith " = to use it as a covering for the faults and follies of others.

Its *Kibleh* (point to which the attention is turned, or Mekka) = the *Pir*.

Its " Ablution " = the cleansing from sin.

Its " Obligation " = the forsaking of cupidity.

Its " Duty " = Contentment.

Its " Soul " = the keeping of vows.

[1] The eighth Imām.

The different parts of this garment have also their several significations. Its border is symbolical of the condition of a Dervish ; its collar, of submission ; its exterior signifies " spiritual light," and its interior " secrecy." The collar and edges are embroidered with Arabic words signifying " O Friend!" " O Healer !" " O Great One!" etc.

The short tight-sleeved vest worn under the mantle is also decorated with twelve stripes of a colour different from the material, likewise symbolising the twelve Imāms.

The girdle worn folded round the waist under the mantle is made from the wool of the sheep sacrificed at the initiation of its owner, and is characterised by several symbolical names. The Bektāshi Dervishes relate that its prototype was worn by Adam, and subsequently by a succession of sixteen Prophets, beginning with Seth, and including Elias, Jesus, and Mohammed. Their legend also says that the one presented to the Prophet by the Angel Gabriel bore the inscription : " There is no God but Allah, Mohammed is His Prophet, and Ali is His Friend." The *kamberieh* is the rope placed round the neck of the Dervish at his initiation, and subsequently worn by him round his waist. Three knots are tied in it, called respectively the *hand-tie*, the *tongue-tie*, and the *rein-tie*, to remind the wearer of his vows of truth, honesty, and chastity. It is also com-memorative of the cord with which Kamber, the groom of the Khalif Ali, was in the habit of tethering his master's horse, " Dūldūl," and serves to support a septagonal crystal, or stone, called the *Palenk*, symbolising " the seven heavens and seven earths, seven seas and seven planets," which, according to the Koran, obey Allah's command and worship him by revolving round His holy seat. Another stone, called the " Stone of Submission " (*teshem tāsh*) is worn suspended round the neck, and attached to it is the following curious legend :—

" Moses, the Servant of God, was in the habit of bathing in the Nile at a spot remote from that used by his fellows for that purpose, in order that they might not observe the radiance that emanated from his body. The evil-minded took advantage of this custom of the Seer to circulate a report that he was leprous, or afflicted with elephantiasis, and for that reason was ashamed to wash with them. ' But Allah cleared him from the scandal which they had spoken concerning him.' [1] One day when Moses was bathing, he laid his clothes on a stone by the riverside. The stone immediately set off at a rapid pace towards Misr (Cairo), followed by the Seer, who, eager in the chase after his garments, found himself amid the Israelites before he was aware. When he came up with the stone, in his wrath he perforated it with his stick in twelve places. The stone then spake and said, ' O Moses, I walked by the command of the Lord, and was the cause that thy purity has been witnessed by the people.' Moses, being sorry for his unjust behaviour,

[1] *Koran*, Chap. xxxiii.

said, ' I have perforated thee in twelve places, for which I ask thy forgiveness—*A Dervish is forgiven by Dervishes*.' [1] ' Well, Moses,' replied the stone, ' I am satisfied with thy excuses ; but now take a cord, and pass it through one of the holes, and keep me till thou requirest a collar of penitence.' Moses did as the stone commanded, and suspended it round his neck." " And this," says the Dervish Evliya, " is the origin of the stones generally worn by Dervishes, and also of that put on by penitents, both of which are called *sigil tashi*." According to the same author, this is the stone that spake to Moses at the rock of Horeb : " O Moses, put me on the ground, and give me twelve blows," upon which twelve streams gushed out of the holes.

Another legend says that the " Stone of Submission " had its origin with Abū Bekr, who, having one day used language which gave offence to the Prophet, repented of his fault, and, to guard against its repetition, hung round his neck a pebble, which he placed in his mouth on entering the mosque.

When putting on for the first time the " Stone of Submission," the Dervish utters this prayer :—

" O Allah, the rites of the Brethren have become my faith ; no doubt now exists in my heart. As I hang round my neck the *teshem tāsh*, I give myself to Thee. In the name of Allah, the Merciful, and the Clement." Then follows the recitation of the

---

[1] This reputed saying of Moses has remained a current expression in the mouth of Dervishes.

chapter of the Koran relative to the striking of the rock by Moses.

A stone of a crescent shape called the *mengoosh tāsh* is also worn as an earring. It is supposed to represent the shoe of Ali's horse "Dūldūl." A Dervish who wears it in only one ear is called a *Hassani ;* one who wears it in both, a *Hussaini*— these terms referring to the two sons of Ali. The wearing of these earrings signifies that the Dervish accepts the words of his spiritual Guide as those of Allah, and that they are the laws that he hangs perpetually over his heart. When he inserts them, he prays : " End of all increase ; Ring about the neck of all prosperity ; Token of those who are in Paradise ; Gift of the Martyr Shah (Hussein) ! Cursed be Yezīd ! " (his murderer).

The *post* or *postaki*, the sheepskin mat on which the Dervish sits, has also its attributes. Its *head* signifies " Submission " ; its *feet*, " Service " ; the *right side*, the " Hand " given to a brother at his initiation ; the *left*, " Honour " ; the *east*, " Secrecy" ; the *west* " Religion " ; the *middle*, " Love." It has also, among other symbols, its *Law*, which means absorption into the Divine Love, when the soul is freed from the body, and wanders away to join other sympathetic spirits.

A curved stick called the *chellek* is kept in the Bektāshi *Tekkehs* for the chastisement of erring Dervishes. It is commemorative of that used by the Khalif to chastise his groom, Kamber, who thenceforth humbly carried it in his girdle.

A curiously shaped instrument called the *tebber* has been mentioned as used by the Bektāshis at their ceremonies of initiation, when it is carried by one of the " Interpreters," or sponsors. The members of this Order carry also a horn in shape like that of a wild goat, and a two-beaked almsbowl. The former is sounded in the *Tekkehs* to call the Brethren to their meals and devotions, and is used generally as a signal from one Dervish to another. It appears to be an imitation of that said to be carried by the Angel Gabriel, and is also called by one of the attributes of the Deity—" O Loving "—and a Bektāshi carrying it makes use of that exclamation.

The cap of the Rūfa'i, or, as they are commonly termed by Europeans, the " Howling " Dervishes, is very similar in form and material to that worn by the Bektāshi Order, and is also called a " Crown." It is of undyed felt, but divided into eight, instead of twelve grooves, each signifying the renunciation of a sin—or what they conceive to be such. The " Crowns " of their Sheikhs are, however, divided into twelve grooves which have the same symbolism as those of the Bektāshis, and their turbans are black.

The mantles of the Rūfa'i Order may be of any colour, but are always bordered with green. The reason for this is given in the following somewhat vapid little legend : " The Prophet once, on receiving some good tidings from the Angel Gabriel, started up and turned round so suddenly that his green mantle fell off his shoulders. His disciples (with his consent, presumably) took possession of the mantle, tore it into shreds, and sewed them round the edges of their own garments. As the Prophet frequently wore a black *khirka*, the Sheikhs of this Order often follow his example." [1]

The knives, red-hot irons and coals, and other instruments used by the Rūfa'i Order in their extraordinary religious exercises, are called by the symbolic name of "Roses." [2] This is evidently connected with the rose-symbolism of the Kadiri Order, whose *Pir* or founder, Abdul Kādr Ghilāni, was, as above mentioned, the uncle and spiritual teacher of the *Pir* of the Rūfa'i Dervishes.

The Kādiri Rose, embroidered on the "Crowns" of the Brethren of that Order, is to them full of mystic meaning. Tradition says that the Prophet bestowed the name of his "Two Roses" on his grandsons, Hasan and Hussain ; and the Sheikhs of

[1] Tradition relates that the Prophet, at his death, bequeathed his mantle to the Dervish Sheikh Uwais, referred to on p. 2. It is said to be a long robe of woollen material made with a collar, and wide sleeves reaching to the knee. The charge of this sacred garment has ever since remained in the family of Uwais. Some years ago when the hereditary guardian of this sacred relic happened to be a minor, a *Vakīl*, or deputy, was appointed by the Sultan to discharge this duty. The mantle is enshrined in one of the buildings comprised within the Old Serai at Stamboul, where it is "venerated " by the Sultan and his Court on the occasion of the annual festival of the *Khirka Shereef*, and also on the occasion of important national events.

[2] To speak of wounds as "flowers " is a common figure of speech with Eastern poets. Compare, for instance, Gibb, *Ottoman Poetry*, p. 240.

the Order, who all claim descent from the family of Mohammed, are credited with the possession of peculiar powers in connection with this flower.[1]

According to a legend of this Order, its *Pir* was directed by Khidhr[2] to proceed to Bagdad and there take up his abode. On arriving at that city Abdul Kādr received from the resident Sheikh a cup filled to the brim with water, which signified that the place was already full of holy men, and that there was consequently no room for him. Replying in the same symbolic language, the Saint miraculously created a rose—it was mid-winter—and placed it in the cup, which did not even then overflow. When this was carried back to the resident Sheikh, he and those with him read the message : " There is yet room in Bagdad for the Kādiri Rose." Marvelling at the miracle, they exclaimed, " The Sheikh Abdul Kādr is our Rose ! " and going out to meet their saintly guest, they conducted him into the city with every mark of respect.

The conventional rose of the *Kādiri* has eighteen petals arranged in three rings of five, six, and seven respectively, and its colours are yellow, red, white and black. The five petals are symbolical of the " five virtues " attributed by the *Pir* of the Order

---

[1] Sulieman Effendi's work on the *Mevlad*, or Birth of the Prophet, contains the following couplet in reference to Abdūl Kādr :—

Whenever he perspired, each drop became a rose,
Each drop, as down it rolled, was gathered as a
treasure.

[2] See above, p. 22.

to the followers of Islam ; the six are symbolical of the six characteristics of faith ; and the seven refer to the seven verses of the *Fatiha*, the first chapter of the Koran, which is also denominated, among other honourable titles, the " Holy Crown," and the " Mother of the Koran."

The *Hamzavi* Order appear to have no distinctive costume, neither do they make use of any mystical symbols in their worship. On their tombstones, however, are sculptured peculiar signs consisting of single and double triangles, with dots above and below the angles, and the " Solomon's Seal " of six points, without the dots.

The Dervish *tesbeh*, or Rosary, consists of ninety-nine beads, the number of the " Beautiful names of Allah " ; and as a Dervish invokes each one of these in his *Zikr*, he records it upon his beads. The rosary is also divided into three equal parts, each of which signifies a formula of worship.

The foregoing are, so far as it is possible to ascertain, the chief among the emblematical meanings connected with the costumes worn and the objects used by the various Orders. They, however, by no means exhaust the list. For, to quote again from Evliya Effendi, " a Dervish's dress is covered without and within with a thousand and one symbols which give occasion for a thousand and one questions. He who is capable of answering them all is a Master of the Science of Mysticism, a true Ascetic, and an Ocean of Knowledge."

CHAPTER VIII

THE VARIOUS RELIGIOUS EXERCISES

" Each Saint and Seer a sacred rite has all his own ;
  Yet, as each rite to Allah leads, their rites are one."
                    JELĀLŪ-'D-DĪN. The *Mesnevi*.

" Mystical dance, which yonder starry sphere
  Of planets, and of fixed, in all her wheels
  Resembles nearest."
                    MILTON. *Paradise Lost*, v, 620-2.

THE religious exercises of the Dervishes may be
said to be, speaking generally, of but two varieties,
the Vocative and the Contemplative. The Orders
which follow the Vocative form claim descent from
the original congregation of the Khalif Ali ; and
their authority for this mode of worship they profess
to find in the Prophet's injunction : " *Call loudly
and without ceasing on the name of Allah !* " given,
tradition says, in reply to his nephew's enquiry as
to what he ought to do in order to obtain Divine
assistance. The Contemplative Orders, who claim
descent from the Brotherhood of Abū Bekr, the
Prophet's uncle, quote, on the other hand, Mohammed's injunction to him when they were concealed
together in a cave during the Flight, to recite
mentally the *Zikr*, or invocation of the Divine Name.
The exercises of many of the leading Orders, however, and especially of those who follow the vocative
form of worship, present other, and even more

marked dissimilarities.   The services of the Mevlevi, Rūfai, and a few of the other Orders are public, and even foreigners, who are rarely admitted into the mosques at the hours of prayer, are courteously welcomed in the *Tekkehs* of such Orders.   The devotions of the rest are performed strictly in private, and do not, indeed, appear to be of a character attractive to outsiders.

The Mevlevi Order is distinguished by its peculiar dance, which differs entirely from the religious exercises of the rest of the Dervishes.   The accompaniment to this sacred dance of instrumental and vocal music is said to have been introduced by the founder of the Order, Jelālū-'d-Dīn ; but dancing, or twirling, by Dervishes had evidently a much more ancient origin, as mention of it occurs in the " Thousand Nights and a Night."   The number of brethren taking part in the ceremony is usually from fifteen to thirty, including the musicians.   When the latter, wearing their tall hats and long cloaks, have taken their places in the gallery, the rest of the fraternity, similarly dressed, their dancing skirts being tucked up and covered by their mantles, enter the *Tekkeh* barefooted, and seat themselves to the left of the doorway on the strip of carpet that borders the octagonal, or circular central space.   The Sheikh, who wears in addition a green turban round his *kulah*, advances to a small prayer-mat opposite his disciples, and the service begins at once with the *Namaz*—the devotions performed five times daily by all good Moslems.   The Sheikh then invites the brethren to join him in reciting the *Fatiha* in these words : " Let us chant the *Fatiha,* glorifying the holy name of Allah, in honour of the blessed religion of the Prophets, but, above all, of Mohammed Mustapha, the greatest, the most august, the most magnificent of all the celestial envoys, and in memory also, of the first four Khalifs (then follows a list of names of the family of the Prophet, the *Pir,* and other holy men). Let us pray for the constant prosperity of our holy society, for the preservation of the very learned and venerable Chelebi Effendi, [1] our Master and Lord ; for the preservation of the Sultan, the very majestic and clement Emperor of the faith of Islam ; for the prosperity of the Grand Vizier, and the Sheikh-ul-Islam, and that of all Mohammedan armies, and of all pilgrims to the holy city of Mekka. Let us pray for the repose of the souls of all the *Pirs* and of all the Dervishes of all other Orders ; for all good people, for all those who have been distinguished for their good works, their foundations [of charitable establishments], and their acts of beneficence. Let us also pray for the Moslems of both sexes in the East and the West, for the maintenance of all prosperity, for the prevention of all adversity, for the accomplishment of all salutary vows, and for the success of all praiseworthy enterprises. Let us finally beseech Allah to deign to preserve us in the gift of His grace, and in the fire of Holy Love."

The Dervishes then chant the *Fatiha* : " Praise

[1] The General of the Order.

be to Allah, the Lord of all creatures, the Most Merciful, the King of the Day of Judgment. Thee do we worship, and of Thee do we beg assistance. Direct us in the right way, in the way of those to whom Thou hast been gracious, and not of those against whom Thou art incensed, nor of those who go astray." This is followed by a prayer to the *Pir* asking for his intercession with Allah and the Prophet. The Sheikh then steps off his prayer-mat, and, standing to the right of it, bows low in reverence to the *Pir*, by whom it is believed to be now occupied. Taking a step forward, he twists himself round, and, standing to the left of the mat, he bows again. He then resumes his former place, and one of the brethren in the orchestra chants a hymn in praise of the Prophet which is followed by a performance by the orchestra.

An elder, called the *Semâ Zân*—who, like the Sheikh, retains his cloak all through the ceremony and does not join in the *devr*, or turning—now leaves his place among the Dervishes and approaches his Superior. Standing with his right great toe crossed over the left, and his arms crossed on his breast, he bows first to the right then to the left of the Sheikh, kisses his hand, and then takes up his position in the centre of the hall. The rest of the brethren, who have in the meantime risen to their feet, taken off their cloaks and let fall their skirts, now advance in single file. Following the example of the *Semâ Zân*, they bow to the right and left of the Sheikh's prayer mat, with crossed toes, arms folded, and hands grasping their shoulders, and then kiss the hand of their Master, who in return bestows a kiss on their *kulahs*. This done, they immediately begin to turn, balancing themselves on the left foot while maintaining a rotatory motion with the right. The Sheikh meanwhile remains standing with devout mien and downcast eyes. Gradually the arms of the dancers are extended ; the right hand is raised with the palm uppermost, and the left lowered with the palm turned downwards. The eyes are closed, and the head inclined on the left shoulder. Mentally reciting the *Zikr* they whirl round the " Hall of Celestial Sounds." The faces of even the youngest members wear an expression of deep serenity as they revolve to the sound of the flutes and drums, a music which appears to have an entrancing effect on those who understand its mystic language. For the Dervish " Lovers of Allah " it expresses the harmony of His creation in which they circle like the stars of the empyrean, isolated from the world in a rapture of spiritual love and communion with Him.

Some of the younger Dervishes spin very rapidly. At the *Mevleh Khaneh* at Salonica I used to remark particularly two neophytes, evidently under eighteen years of age, who were extraordinarily proficient in this exercise ; but some of the older brethren turned very slowly and feebly. None, however, showed any signs of fatigue or giddiness. When the *devr* has continued for some ten or fifteen minutes, the *Semâ Zân* gives the signal for its discontinuance by stamping with one thinly-shod foot on the floor. The Dervishes, as a rule, all stop at the same instant like the wheels of a machine, and, very curiously, all in a circle with their faces turned towards the Sheikh, though sometimes one or two, more absorbed than the rest in their mystic ecstasy, fail to hear the signal, which has sometimes to be repeated more than once. Crossing their arms on their breasts, and grasping their shoulders, they bow low to their superior, and then, falling into single file, pass before him with the same reverences as before, and re-commence their gyrations. This exercise is usually repeated a third time, after which the Dervishes resume their seats on the floor, and cover themselves with their mantles. The service concludes with recitations from the Koran, and the customary prayer for the Sultan.

Each *Tekkeh* has a particular day, or days, in the week for the public performances of the brethren, and, in places like Constantinople, where there are several communities belonging to the same Order, the Dervishes visit and take part in each other's ceremonies. Nothing, however, forbids a Dervish to take part in the religious exercises of another Order, save want of the necessary practice and skill. If a Kādiri, for instance, can perform the *devr* of the Mevlevi Order, he has only to apply to the superintendent of the *Tekkeh* for a costume and is welcome to enter the hall with the brethren.

Among the Rūfai, Kādiri, Khalveti, Bairami,

Gulshani, Ushaki and some other Orders, the *devr* consists in the Dervishes holding each other by the hand, or pressing closely together, and increasing the movements of their bodies at every step they take in making the round of the hall. A performer may disengage himself from the circle and desist from the *devr* at any moment he pleases ; but those gifted with greater powers of endurance and more enthusiastic temperaments strive by their exertions to excite the rest. These take off their " crowns "— which they hand to the Sheikh—form an inner circle, entwine their arms and press their shoulders together, repeating incessantly *Yā Allah !* or *Yā Hoo !* until compelled by sheer exhaustion to desist.

The Rūfai Order not only exceed the others in the violence of their exercises, but use also in their frenzy knives, fire, and hot irons. The opening ritual is the same as that of the generality of the Orders, but the services last longer, and are divided into five distinct ceremonies, some of which are peculiar to this Order. The Sheikh is seated on a sheepskin mat in front of the *kibleh*—the niche in the wall which indicates the direction of Mekka— and the service opens with acts of homage performed before him. Four of the elders first approach, embrace each other, and seat themselves two on either side of their superior. The other Dervishes then come forward one by one, with crossed arms and bowed heads. They first salute the name of the Founder engraved on a tablet of stone over the *kibleh*, pass both their hands over their faces and beards, and, kneeling in turn before the Superior, kiss his hand, and then proceed to their places on the sheepskin mats spread in a horse-shoe design in front of him. All now chant the *Tekbir* and the *Fatiha*. This concluded, the Sheikh pronounces the first attribute of the Deity, repeating it incessantly while the disciples respond *Allah! Allah!* swaying themselves from side to side and placing their hands in turn on various parts of their bodies. One of the elders then commences the second half of the service by chanting a hymn in praise of the Prophet, the Dervishes meanwhile continuing their repetition of the *Zikr;* now, however, moving their bodies backwards and forwards. After a while they spring to their feet, and stand close together, swaying by a movement of the whole body from side to side, and then again backwards and forwards, all observing an exact rhythm in their exercise, and continuing the ejaculation of *Allah! Allah!* varied occasionally by that of *Yā Hoo!* (" O Him! "). They now appear violently agitated, sigh and sob, shed tears, and perspire profusely ; their eyes are closed, their faces pale, and their expression and demeanour languid in the extreme.

The third scene commences to the sound of an *Ilāhi*, or mystical song composed by one of the many canonised Sheikhs of this Order. While it is being sung by two of the elders, the most enthusiastic of the brethren places himself in the midst of his fellows, and by his example excites them to a higher

pitch of religious fervour. Should a Dervish belonging to another community happen to be present,
it is considered an act of courtesy to offer him this
office, and should there be several visitors, they
perform it in succession. A Mevlevi, however, is
not expected to perform any but his own *Devr*.

In the fourth scene all the Dervishes lay aside
their turbans, form a circle with arms and shoulders
pressed against each other, and make the circuit of
the hall, alternately striking the floor with their
feet in unison, and springing up in a body. The
two elders continue their chanting, interrupted from
time to time by cries of *Yā Allah!* and *Yā Hoo!*
which increase, when shouted all together, to the
extraordinary sound which has gained for them the
name of the "Howling Dervishes." If at any
moment they appear about to stop from sheer
exhaustion, the Sheikh exhorts them to fresh exertions by placing himself in their midst. The elders
follow suit and outdo the rest in physical agitation,
exciting their emulation by every means in their
power. Two Dervishes now take down from niches
in the wall several sharp-pointed iron instruments,
and, having heated them red hot in a brazier, present
them to the Sheikh. And now commences the final
scene.

The Sheikh recites prayers over the instruments,
invokes the name of the *Pir*, breathes upon them,
raises them to his lips, and then presents them to
his disciples. These devotees, excited by their
previous exercises, are now in the state of religious

delirium called *hal*. Some eagerly seize the hot irons, regard them fondly, plunge them into their flesh, lick them, or hold them in their mouths ; and all without evincing any sign of pain, but rather as if intoxicated by the perfume of the " Rose of Bagdad," of which they are said to be mystically symbolical. [1] Others seize daggers from their resting-places on the walls, or hot coals from the brazier, with which they cut or burn their flesh. Some fall, overcome by their excitement, into the arms of their brethren ; and all finally sink, exhausted and unconscious, on the floor. The Sheikh presently walks among them, whispers in their ears a mystical word that recalls them to consciousness, breathes upon them, and anoints their wounds with his saliva. It is said, and indeed commonly believed by the Mohammedan spectators, that all traces of their hurts disappear within twenty-four hours. A Rūfai legend says that their founder, Ahmed Saïd Rūfai, having on one occasion put his legs in a pan of live coals, his burns were immediately healed by the *nefs* (breath) and saliva of his uncle, Abdul Kādr Ghilāni, who at the same time endowed with his healing power the Rūfai *Pir*.

The *Devr* of the Sādi Order is similar to that just described, but leads to no self-mutilations. It consists chiefly of violent changes of attitude and physical agitation, continued until the devotees finally fall exhausted and unconscious.

The Kādiris, after reciting the *Fatiha* already

[1] See above, p. 119.

described, take each other by the shoulders and
turn in a circle round the hall of their *Tekkeh*. This
variety of the *devr* was not originated by the
founder of the Order, but was adopted at the
instance of one of its most eminent Sheikhs.

Among the "contemplative" Dervishes the
Bektāshis are the most numerous. Their devotions,
after the customary recitations, are conducted in
silence, a form of worship known as the *Hiffi*.

The service of the Nakshibendi Order consists of
one prayer called the *Iklah*, repeated a thousand and
one times. This number of pebbles is distributed
among the brethren who are seated in a circle
on the floor ; and, as each one completes the mental
recitation of an *Iklah*, he lays down before him a
pebble until the whole number are deposited
within the circle.

The Hamzavis, or as they are also called, Melami-
youns, appear to have in former centuries maintained great secrecy with regard to their religious
rites—a fact that not unnaturally gave rise to
suspicions of their orthodoxy. They were accused
of belonging to the Order of Freemasons,[1] and, as
related in a subsequent chapter,[2] were subjected to
active persecution. To judge, however, from their
Litany, they appear to be a singularly pious sect,
and they enjoy the reputation of being most con-
scientious in all their dealings, living only for

[1] The term *Fermason* = "Freemason," is, among
orthodox Moslems, synonymous with "infidel."
[2] Below, p. 186.

their doctrines, regardless of the things of this world.

The following account of their rites and principles from the writings of Abdul Baki, a Dervish of the Order, is quoted from Mr. Brown's *The Dervishes* [1] :—

"Whenever those who follow in this path, and who love the unique God, to the number of two or three, or more, are about to meet together and join in the *tevheed* and the *zikr*, and their hearts are occupied with their worldly affairs, they should, on their way to the place of meeting, employ their minds with thoughts of God, in all sincerity and purity, and also beg their *Pir* to lend them his spiritual aid, so that when they reach the place of meeting they may all, small and great, with humility and contrition, embrace the hand of each other, and devoutly join in the contemplation of the Deity, and turn their faces towards the Grace of the All-Just, the ever rising Love of Allah, without harbouring in the tongue, in the mind, or otherwise, any thoughts respecting worldly concerns, but, with perfect hearts and active spirits, take part in these pious ceremonies.

"They must next offer up those prayers which are conformable with the rules of the Order, seat themselves, and, if there be among them anyone possessing a pleasing voice, let him read aloud ten verses of the great Koran, and interest the congregation with some account of the Prophets and Saints, or

[1] P. 182.

even of the Deity. No one must feel concern about his worldly affairs, but the remarks of all must relate to the Love of Allah, or tend to pious fervour. No one not belonging to the Order must be admitted, for, should any such be present, the peculiar gift of God (*Faiz Ullah*) will not be vouchsafed."

The aim of the Nakshibendi Order, in the performance of their *zikr*, is to detach the senses completely from worldly surroundings. The Sheikh and his disciples sit facing each other, the former mentally reciting the invocation, while each of the brethren endeavours to keep his attention fixed by placing his heart in imagination in view of that of his Master, closes his eyes and lips, presses his tongue against the roof of his mouth, and so regulates his breathing that between each respiration he can mentally repeat three times the *zikr*.

As already mentioned,[1] the Order of the Nakshibendi was a revival of the original fraternity of Abū Bekr which, by the successful establishment of other Orders, had become extinct. The Brotherhood meet once a week, generally on a Thursday at sunset, the hour of the fifth *Namāz* or daily prayer. In each city, suburb, or quarter (*mahallāh*) the members of this religious society assemble at the houses of their respective Sheikhs, where, seated round the room on the divan, they perform their devotions. The Superior, or one of the fraternity, chants the prayers, and the assembly responds *Hoo!* or *Allah!* In some cities, however, this

[1] Above, p. 17.

Order possesses special *Tekkehs* in which their services are held ; and in these cases their Sheikh is distinguished from his congregation by a turban similar to that worn by the *Imāms* who officiate in the mosques.

CHAPTER IX

SURVIVALS OF PAGANISM

" The talisman of magic might,
Hid in some ruin's lonely site,
Emerges from its ancient night
At the mild glance of Dervishes."

HAFIZ.

CONSIDERING that the existence of magic and witchcraft, and the power of the " Evil Eye " are stated as absolute facts in the Koran, it is not surprising that in Mohammedan countries superstitious beliefs and practices play so great a part in the social life of the people. For to deny the existence of magicians and enchantments would be tantamount to denying the authenticity of the Holy Book ; and a devout Moslem, even if sufficiently enlightened to discredit the popular superstitions that meet him at every turn, is constrained to admit that magic *was* practised on the very person of the Prophet. The words made use of as counter-spells, and exorcisms are, indeed, taken chiefly from the two chapters of the Koran relating to magic and malevolence, and beginning :—

" Say, I fly for refuge unto the Lord of the Daybreak, that he may deliver me from the mischief of those things which He hath created, and from the mischief of the night when it cometh on, and from the mischief of women blowing on knots, and from the mischief of the envious when he envieth," etc.[1]

Commentators on the Koran relate that the reason for the revelation of these chapters was that a Jew named Lobeid, had, with the assistance of his daughters, bewitched Mohammed by tying eleven knots in a cord which they hid in a well. The Prophet falling ill in consequence, this chapter and that following it were revealed ; and the Angel Gabriel acquainted him with the use he was to make of them, and told him where the cord was hidden. The Khalif Ali fetched the cord, and the Prophet repeated over it these two chapters ; at every verse a knot was loosed, till, on finishing the last words, he was entirely freed from the charm.[2]

In the chapter on Convents and Shrines I have described a somewhat similar operation performed by a Mevlevi Dervish at the tomb of St. Dimitri. In this case, however, the knots were evidently made with the object of " tying up " sickness and other ills.

The ignorant among the Moslems of Turkey, in

[1] *Koran*, Surah cxiii.

[2] In a note to this chapter in his translation Mr. Sale says that the words " blowing on knots " refer to " witches who used to tie knots and to blow upon them, uttering at the same time certain magical words over them in order to work on or debilitate the person they had a mind to injure." In the same note it is stated that " this was a common practice in former days—what they call in France *nouer l'éguillette*—and the knots which the wizards in the northern parts tie when they sell mariners a wind are relics of the same superstition."

common, it must be admitted, with the native
Christians and Jews, attribute the majority of the
ills the flesh is heir to, and also misfortunes generally, to the influence of magic; and, consequently,
have recourse to the same mysterious agency for
their cure. By the populace the Dervishes are held
to be experts in the magic of the old Paganism,
belief in which is thus sanctioned by their Holy
Book. They are, indeed, credited with the faculty
not only of healing mental and bodily diseases, but
also of counteracting the effects of witchcraft and
sorcery, of interpreting dreams, recovering lost or
stolen property, and even of restoring to wives the
waning affection of their husbands. When anyone
falls ill, the women of the family—for it need hardly
be said that the firmest believers in this mode of
spiritual cure are of the female sex—send for some
saintly Sheikh to remove the spell which has caused
the ailment, or, at least, to counteract its influence.
This holy man, whose breath, sanctified by the
constant repetition of the Divine Name (*Zikr*), has
acquired a supernaturally healing power, breathes
on the head and afflicted parts of the patient, laying
at the same time his hands upon him. This concluded, he produces a tiny scroll of paper inscribed
with some sacred words, or a passage from the Koran,
which he orders to be either swallowed by the sufferer,
soaked in water and the liquid drunk, or worn on
the person for a stated number of days. It is
recorded in the *Mesnevi* that Jelálü-'d-Din made
use of this remedy to cure a disciple suffering from

intermittent fever. The potion was accompanied
by the following supplication in which the malady
is personalised and addressed by a propitiatory
title :—

" O Mother of the Sleek One ! If thou hast believed
in Allah, the Most High, make not the head to
ache, pollute not the throat, devour not the flesh,
drink not the blood, and depart thou out of ——,
betaking thyself to one who attributes to Allah
partners of other false gods. And I testify that
there is no god but God, and that Mohammed is
His Servant and Apostle." [1]

Among other exorcisms, the use of which is said
to have originated at the time of Mohammed,
it is related by the historian, Ahmet Effendi, that,
in the tenth year of the Hegira, the Khalif Ali being
about to march against the province of Yemen, the
army of which far outnumbered his own, expressed
some anxiety as to the success of the expedition.
To reanimate the courage of his nephew, the Prophet
put his own turban on the head of Ali, and pressed
his hands on his breast, saying, " O Allah, purify
his tongue, strengthen his heart, and direct his
mind ! " Religious tradition has exaggerated the
importance of these words until they have come to
be considered the source from which the exorcising

---

[1] The smallpox is similarly designated by the Greeks
" the Blessing," and by the Dyaks of Borneo " the Chief."
The Greeks have many similar exorcisms. See Polites,
Αἱ 'Ασθένειαι κατὰ τοὺς μύθους τοῦ 'Ελληνικοῦ λαοῦ, in the Δελτίον
τῆς 'Ιστορικῆς καὶ 'Εθνολογικῆς 'Εταιρίας Vol. I.   One of these has
been given in my *Greek Folk-poesy*, Vol. II.

Sheikhs derive the virtue and efficacy of their spiritual
remedies.

Cabalistic talismans prepared by Dervishes
are also in great request as preventives against, as
well as cures for, real and imaginary calamities, and
are constantly worn attached to the head-dress, or
hung round the neck. The efficacy of the scrolls
just described, which are called by the various
names of *nushka*, *yafta*, and *hammaïl*, can only be
relied upon, according to the Sheikhs who prescribe
them, when administered by their own hands. But
whatever the success of these remedies may be in
individual cases, nothing can shake popular belief
in their general efficacy. If the patient is not bene-
fited by them, the fault naturally lies in his want
of faith, or in the neglect of some other condition.
The holy man, in any case, receives an honorarium
for his services, either in coin or in kind ; but if a
speedy cure is the result of his ministrations, his
reward will be large in proportion.

The Dervishes, in common with all Orientals,
attach great sacredness to the thirty-four letters of
the Arabic Alphabet, and assign to each a numerical
value. Of this mode of thinking we have a familiar
illustration in the Apocalyptic puzzle of the name
of the seven-headed beast which " is the number
of a man ; and his number is six hundred and three
score and six," [1] a puzzle of which the true solution
has been shown to be Νέρων Καῖσαρ, the value of
which letters, transcribed in Hebrew, is 666. Most

[1] Rev. xiii, 18.

persistent, too, have been the superstitious notions
with regard to numbers.   We find that in 1666, the
Jews, not only in the East, but in many parts of
Europe, were so confident of the appearance of the
Messiah that the Jewish imposter, Shabathaï Shévi,
found himself surrounded by disciples in every town
in which he announced his Messiahship.   And that,
even in England at the present day, belief in the
" magic of figures " is not extinct is evident from a
paragraph which appeared in a London newspaper
at the beginning of 1888, recording the eventful
character to this country of former years whose three
final figures were alike, and suggesting that the
same being the fact in 1888 " is itself portentous."[1]
The numerical values of the Arabic alphabet are
made use of to draw up a class of talismans of a
mystical and cabalistic character by means of what
the Dervishes call the " Science of Calculation."
Chronograms are written according to the same
system, and in many of the inscriptions on public
edifices, the last line, though written in the same
character as the rest, and expressing in connection
with them some poetical idea, will be found, on
calculation, to give also the date of its composition.
Eminent Dervishes were often commanded by the
early Sultans to compose such inscriptions as
" talismans" for the gateways of conquered towns, or
newly-erected public buildings.   Hadji Bektāsh is
said to have composed many of these inscriptions,
and, very curiously, the letters forming his name

[1] *Pall Mall Gazette*, Jan. 5, 1888.

give at the same time the date of the foundation of his Order.

Talismanic charms are also often composed, among other methods, of cabalistic calculations based on the numerical value of the letters composing the name of the person interested. In a divination for the purpose of fortune-telling, these values are multiplied and divided, and their cubes and squares added and subtracted according to some conventional formula, to obtain a result, odd or even. If even, it is considered lucky; if odd, the reverse.

The idea of the sacred and mysterious character of letters has also given rise to a belief that each one has its special attendant *Djin* appointed by Allah to wait upon it, and that these *Djins* may be invoked either severally or collectively. In order to secure the invisible presence of these " Slaves of the Letter," the calculations must be drawn up on certain days and hours, and at certain periods of the moon and positions of the stars. Such cabalistic figures are also frequently engraved on stones brought from the holy cities of Mekka, Medina, or Damascus, or from the neighbourhood of the tombs of holy men such as Hadji Bektāsh, or Hadji Bairām. Sometimes, however, these amulets are inscribed with a verse from the Koran, or an invocation addressed to the Prophet or the Khalif Ali. When a charm is concocted for the purpose of inspiring someone with the tender passion, the *Djins* invoked by it are believed to meet in council in order to devise a series of influences which will compel the person aimed at to obey them. The only antidote against such a charm is to draw up one that will ensure another assembly of *Djins* who will either overcome the first, or compel them to agree to a compromise, and so release the victim from their influence. Some of the talismans purchased from these Dervish magicians are credited with the power of procuring the visits of beneficent *Djins* who cure the suffering in body, ease the troubled in mind, and grant the desires of the person invoking their aid. Other charms are believed to influence dreams when placed under the pillow of one asleep.

The four elements are also credited with the possession of twenty-eight letters having numerical values ranging from one to a thousand. They are divided into four classes of seven each, and to each class is attributed a " temperament " according to the nature of the element its letters represent. To the letters representing water is given the predominance over all the others, as, in accordance with the Mohammedan account of the creation, water was the original element, and from it the other three were created.[1] Calculations are made to discover which of the four elements exists in too large a proportion in the system of a suffering person ; and when this has been discovered, a charm (*nushka*) is drawn up, which, swallowed or worn next to the skin, will enable the patient to get rid of the superabundant element.

[1] Sales' *Koran*, Chap. xli, p. 356, n.

The Dervishes are also often had recourse to for the recovery of lost or stolen property. Sheikh Ali, the head of the Bektāshi fraternity at Salonica before mentioned, [1] enjoyed a great reputation for success in this particular line of his profession. His mode of procedure was to ascertain the names of all the persons who had visited a house where any such loss had been sustained and visit each in turn. While gossiping about the event he would let drop a hint that the guilty person would be made the object of some magical charm if he did not at once restore the property to its owner; and, superstitious fear getting the better of cupidity, the lost article would usually be recovered as mysteriously as it had disappeared. The skill of this Dervish as an interpreter of dreams was also said to rival that of a famous Turkish witch in the city. I happened on the occasion of one of his visits to have had my sleep disturbed on the previous night by a dream of green snakes, and took the opportunity of asking for his explanation of it. Divining, no doubt, that I was not of a credulous or superstitious turn of mind, he merely replied, with a shrug of the shoulders and a graceful gesture of the hands, "*Eyei olsoun!*" (May it be good).

Dervishes figure not infrequently in Oriental folk-tales, both Moslem and Christian. Everyone is acquainted with the " One-eyed Kalender " of the *Thousand Nights and a Night*, though few, perhaps, recognise in the bearer of that appellation a wandering

[1] Above, p. 40.

Dervish. In Greek folk-tale, Dervishes are often credited with the possession of magical objects such as cups that are instantly filled with whatever the owner may desire ; knives that slay man or beast at his command ; reed-flutes, the sound of which brings the dead to life ; turbans of invisibility, etc., etc.[1] Stories are also current of secret hoards of wealth wrested by Dervish Sheikhs, deeply versed in magic, from the guardianship of *Djins* who had possessed them from time immemorial in their subterranean palaces.

[1] Compare, for instance, *Greek Folk-poesy*, " The Story of the Soothsayer," Vol. II, p. 230.

CHAPTER X

THE ACTS OF THE ADEPTS

"A Saint is aware of every thought of the King's heart, and of every secret on earth or in heaven."—*Saying of* JELĀLŪ-'D-DĪN.

As mentioned in previous chapters, the mental and physical condition necessary for the manifestation of their abnormal powers is termed by the Dervishes *Hāl*, a word simply signifying "state." There appear, however, to be two distinct descriptions of *Hāl*, induced by methods of a totally opposite character, and resulting in powers which differ in a corresponding degree.

The first appears to be of a merely temporary nature, and is found only among certain Orders such as the Rūfa'i (" Howling Dervishes ") during their religious exercises performed collectively in the hall of their *Tekkeh*. As has been seen in the chapter on the " Religious Exercises," the devotees, by a contagious emulation, work themselves and each other into an abnormal state of agitation, both mental and physical, during which they inflict upon themselves injuries which, under ordinary conditions, would be dangerous, if not fatal, but which, when inflicted while they are in this strange state of excitement, are, in many cases, not even followed by the loss of a drop of blood, and are mysteriously and speedily healed by the breath and spittle of the Sheikh. That mental states are contagious we have, I think, abundant evidence in cases of panic, when persons, without having the faintest idea of the cause, will excitedly join in the general rush ; and also in so-called Christian " Revivals "—instances of which are, perhaps, more common in America than elsewhere, and especially among the excitable negro population, when, during an enthusiastic " camp meeting," many persons become perfectly frenzied with religious excitement. [1]

The dance (*Devr*) of the Mevlevi Dervishes also produces a species of *Hāl*. It would indeed be difficult to account otherwise for the ability of some twenty men and youths to spin round with closed eyes and outstretched arms within a limited circle for the space of from ten to fifteen minutes without either coming into collision with each other, or showing any signs of giddiness—a scarcely possible feat under ordinary conditions.

The second description of *Hāl*, which appears to be permanent, or, at least, assumable at will, is attained only by those Dervishes who, through long and fervent contemplation of the Deity, have arrived at the Fourth, or highest degree, that of " Union with Allah." Sheikhs and Dervishes of superior grade, belonging to all Orders, whether

---

[1] A curious illustration of this occurred a few years ago in Ottawa, where a series of revivalist services resulted, according to the *Montreal Star*, in the " conversion " of the Premier of the Dominion and his lady, though his name " has so long been the synonym of iniquity in many worthy minds."

Vocative or Contemplative, are equally credited with ability to acquire this degree of sanctity ; and on attaining it they become endowed with various spiritual and superhuman powers. Among these may be named what is termed the " Power of the Will," thought-reading, the gift of prophecy, knowledge of what is happening afar off, and power to influence the event, as also ability to appear in person at great distances for the help of friends or the confusion of enemies, and miracle-working generally. These wonderful gifts can, it is believed, be transmitted by a Sheikh, with his mantle of office, to the disciple who shall prove himself by his rapid advance on the Mystic Path to be a worthy recipient of them, even as Elijah bestowed his mantle on Elisha and endowed him with his own miraculous powers. Instances of the exercise of the Power of the Will are to be found in the biography of every Dervish of renown. In some cases the subject is conscious of the influence under which he is acting, in others he is quite unaware of it, as in the following incident related by the learned Sūfi, Mohammed Bahā-'d-Dīn, of his spiritual Master :—

" In my youth I was ever with Our Lord (Mevlānā) Sa'ed ed Dīn of Kashgar at Hereed. It happened one day, as we were walking out together, that we came upon a number of the people of the place who were engaged in the exercise of wrestling. We agreed together to aid one of the wrestlers so that he might throw his opponent, and afterwards to change our design in favour of the discomfited one.

So we stopped as if to look on, and as we looked, gave the full influence of our united wills to one individual, and he was immediately able to vanquish the other.   Each person we chose in turn vanquished his opponent, and the power of our wills was thus clearly manifested." [1]

This Sheikh also took an active part in the wars of his time between the Sultans of Bokhara and Samarcand; and by means of his wonderful powers is held to have greatly influenced their history. The monarch who took the precaution of securing his goodwill was invariably victorious ; while those who disdained his assistance met with loss and disaster ; and many persons who had wronged the Sheikh or his friends in the troubled times in which he lived felt the weight of his spiritual displeasure. Some even fell sick and died, or recovered only after making full confession and restitution, and obtaining his pardon and intercession with Allah on their behalf.   It was said that he could hold converse with his disciples and friends at a great distance, and their appeals to him were always heard and answered.

Over the minds of his followers Sheikh Sa'ed-'d-Dîn is said to have exercised a peculiar power.   He could influence them in such a way as to throw them at will into a species of trance during which they could remember no single event of their past lives, nor anything they had previously learnt ; and in this state they would remain until their Master

[1] J. P. Brown, *The Dervishes.*

chose to restore to them the possession of their
ordinary faculties. This Power of the Will would
appear to be but a kind of mesmeric influence,
intensified, perhaps, by the complete mental sub-
ordination of a disciple to his spiritual guide.   " Let
your *Mūrshid* be always present to your mind, whatever you are doing or saying," is a primary obligation. And when we consider that, in addition
to this state of constant mental subjection, the
body of the *Murid* is enfeebled by fasting and his
mind fatigued by long vigils and protracted devotions, while his imagination is at the same time
fully impressed with the belief that his Superior is
really in possession of such powers, it is not difficult
to understand that a remarkable ascendancy can
be obtained by a Sheikh over his disciples.   Nothing
indeed could be better adapted to induce suscepti-
bility to hypnotic influences than the discipline to
which a Dervish is subjected during his novitiate.
And having felt in his own person the potency of
the spell of his *Mūrshid*, he will easily be led to
credit him with the faculty of similarly influencing
others.

Not individuals only, however, but crowds have
been known to be affected in this way by eminent
Dervishes ; and according to Moslem legend, even
opposing armies have been caused to desist from
hostilities, completely subdued by the pacificatory
spell thrown over them by some " Man of Peace,"
who has also compelled their leaders to sign treaties
drawn up by himself.   The writings of the Sūfis

teem with traditions and anecdotes recording the marvellous spiritual attainments of those Higher Mystics, and of the resulting abnormal powers exercised by them. Some of these biographies have been translated into European languages, but of others fragments only are available.

Many strange stories are related of Abdūl Kādr of Ghilān, already mentioned as the founder of the Kādiri Order. The poet Sādi records in his "*Gūlistān*" that when visiting the sanctuary of the Ka'aba, the great Sheikh laid his face on the pebbled pavement and prayed : "O Lord ! pardon me ; but if I am deserving of punishment, raise me up at the resurrection blind, that I may not be ashamed in the sight of the righteous." And Sir John Malcolm gives the following legend, translated by him from a Persian MS., concerning this famous Sheikh : "His mother declared that when he was at the breast, he never tasted milk (? from sunrise to sunset) during the holy month of Ramazan ; and in one of his works he gives this account of himself : 'The day before the feast of *Araf*, I went out into the fields and laid hold of the tail of a cow, which turned round and exclaimed, "O Abdūl Kādr, am I not that which thou hast created me ? " I returned home and mounted to the terrace of my house : I saw all the pilgrims standing at the mountain of Arāfūt at Mekka. I went and told my mother that I must dedicate myself to God : I wished to proceed to Bagdad to obtain knowledge. I informed her of what I had seen, and she wept. Then, taking out eighty *deenars*, she told me that, as I had a brother, half of that was all my inheritance. She made me swear when she gave it to me, never to tell a lie ; and then bade me farewell, exclaiming, " Go, my son, I give thee to God. We shall not meet again until the Day of Judgment ! " I went on well till I came to Hamadan, when our Kāffilāh (caravan) was plundered by forty horsemen. One fellow asked me what I had got. " Forty *deenars*," I said, " are sewed under my garment." The fellow laughed, thinking, no doubt, I was joking him. " What have you got ? " asked another. I gave him the same answer. When they were dividing the spoil, I was called to an eminence where their chief stood. " What property have you, my little fellow ? " said he. " I have told two of your people already," I replied, " that I have forty *deenars* sewed up carefully in my clothes." He desired them to be ripped open, and found my money. " And how came you," he asked with surprise, " to declare so openly what has been so carefully hidden ? " " Because," I replied, " I will not be false to my mother whom I have promised that I will never tell a lie." " Child," said the robber, " hast thou such a sense of thy duty to thy mother at thy years ; and am I insensible, at my age, of the duty I owe my God ? Give me thy hand, innocent boy," he continued, " that I may swear repentance on it." He did so. His followers were all alike touched with the scene. " Thou hast been our leader in guilt," said they to the chief, " be the same in the path of virtue," and instantly at his order they made restitution of their spoil, and vowed repentance on my hand.' " [1]

Abdūl Kādr arrived in Bagdad about 1085, and, consequently, when this event happened, he must have been about seventeen years of age. He does not, however, appear to have begun his public lectures until he had reached his fiftieth year. Not only Sūfi writers, but eminent *Sunni,* or orthodox Moslem authorities, record many of his miracles. God granted all his requests, and the Divine vengeance fell on all those who wronged him. He himself gives the following account of the fast he underwent during his probation :—

" I was eleven years in a tower, and when there I vowed to God that I would neither eat nor drink until some one compelled me to do so. I maintained my fast for forty days, after which a person brought me a little meat, put it before me, and went away. My life was nearly springing out of me at the sight of the victuals, but I refrained ; and I heard a voice from within me call out, ' I am hungry, I am hungry ! ' At that moment Sheikh Abū Seyyid Mukzoomī (a celebrated Sūfi) passed, and, hearing the voice, exclaimed, ' What is that ? ' ' It is my mortal part,' I replied, ' but the soul is yet firm, and awaits the result.' ' Come to my house,' he said, and went away. I resolved, however, to fulfil my vow, and remained where I was ; but Elias [2]

[1] *Hist. of Persia,* Vol. II, p. 286, n.
[2] See above, p. 22.

came and told me to follow the Seyyid, whom I found at his door awaiting me. ' You would not comply with my wish,' said he, ' until it was enforced by Elias.' After this he gave me meat and drink in plenty, and then invested me with a *khirka* (mantle) and I became his confirmed friend and companion." [1]

Many and wonderful are the legends which have gathered round the name of the great mystic poet, Jelālū-'d-Dīn. The *Acts of the Adepts*, compiled by Eflāki in the fourteenth century, contains some hundreds of anecdotes concerning Jelāl, his family, friends, and followers, most of which are narratives of supernatural actions performed by living or dead Dervishes, male or female, or of some remarkable event connected with them.

Bāha-'d-Dīn Veled, the father of Jelālū-'d-Dīn, was hardly less famous among the Mystics of the thirteenth century than was his illustrious son ; and besides being closely related to the reigning dynasty of Khorassan, was able to trace his descent to Abū Bekr, the " Commander of the Faithful," and uncle of the Prophet. In virtue of his learning and mystic piety, Bāha-'d-Dīn was held in such high estimation by the inhabitants of the capital, Balkh, as to excite the jealous animosity of the Sultan's courtiers, who accused him of aspiring to the throne. He accordingly quitted the city with a following of about forty souls, after delivering in the great mosque a public address in which he foretold the

[1] Malcolm, *Hist. of Persia*, Vol. II, p. 286, n.

advent of the Moguls and the subversion of the country. Arrived at Bagdad, he was received with great honour by the Khalif, but refused the costly gifts he would have bestowed upon him. Preaching in the mosque, he dared to reprove the monarch to his face for his evil course of life, and foretold that he would be slain by the Moguls under circumstances of great ignominy and cruelty. During Bāha-'d-Dīn's sojourn at Bagdad news came of the conquest of Balkh; he again set out on his travels, and, after various wanderings, was finally invited to Konieh by the Seljūk Sultan, Alā-'d-Dīn, who had made that city his capital. Here Bāha-'d-Dīn was warmly welcomed and liberally entertained by this prince, under whose auspices he established a college, and from whom he received the honourable title of " Sultan of Learned Men " (*Sultan 'l-Ulemā*).

Numerous stories are related of the wonderful spiritual gifts possessed by this illustrious Teacher, and of the great influence he exercised over others, not only during his lifetime, but also after death. One of these relates that when Sultan Alā'u-'d-Dīn had fortified Konieh, he invited Bāha Veled to mount to the terraced roof of the palace, thence to survey the walls and towers. After this inspection Bāha remarked to the Sultan, " Against torrents, and against the horsemen of the enemy, thou hast raised a goodly defence. But what protection hast thou built against those unseen arrows, the sighs and moans of the oppressed, which overleap a thousand walls and sweep whole worlds to destruction ? Go to, now ! strive to acquire the blessings of thy subjects. These are a stronghold compared to which the walls and turrets of the strongest castles are as nothing." [1]

Another anecdote says that shortly after the death of Bāha-'d-Dīn, the Sultan of Kharism, Jelālū-'d-Dīn Shah, arrived on the borders of Asia Minor with a great army. On hearing this alarming news, the Sultan of Konieh went to pray at the tomb of the deceased Sheikh, and then prepared to meet the enemy who were encamped in the neigh-bourhood of Erzerūm. Disguising himself, he set out with a few followers to reconnoitre, and actually entered the enemy's camp. At midnight the sainted Sheikh appeared to him in a dream and warned him to fly. The Sultan awoke, but attaching no import-ance to the warning, went to sleep again. The Saint now appeared a second time. Alā-'d-Dīn saw himself seated on his throne, and the Saint approaching him smote him on the breast with his staff, saying angrily, " Why sleepest thou ? Arise ! " So the Sultan arose, got together his people and horses, and stole from the camp. Not long after-wards the two armies engaged ; the Sultan of Konieh came off victorious ; and in all subsequent difficulties had recourse to the powerful aid of the Saint whom he had in life honoured and befriended.

Jelālū-'d-Dīn, who had studied under the most eminent teachers of Aleppo and Damascus, succeeded

[1] *Acts of the Adepts*, Redhouse's translation, p. 10.

his father as Director of the College at Konieh, and also in the title of " Sultan of Learned Men." The high reputation for piety and learning that the young scholar had already acquired gained for him the devotion of his father's disciples ; and in addition to these he soon gathered around him four hundred enthusiastic students by whom he was designated *Mevlāna* (Our Lord), a title from which, as above mentioned, the Order founded by him took its name.

Eflāki relates the following incident as illustrative of the close friendship and devotion to each other of these Sūfi Saints. An eminent Sheikh, the Seyyid Burhā-nu-'d Dīn [1] had been a pupil of Bāha-'d-Dīn during his residence at Balkh. On his master's departure from that city, the Seyyid went to Termiz, and, after living some time there as a recluse, he began to lecture publicly. During one of his discourses he suddenly stopped and cried out in a tone of anguish, accompanied by floods of tears : " Alas ! my Master has passed away from this Tabernacle of Dust to the Abode of Sincerity ! " His words and the time of their utterance were noted down, and were subsequently found to correspond exactly with the moment of Bāha Veled's death. When the disciples at Termiz had mourned forty days for the great Teacher, the Seyyid said to them, " The son of my master, Jelālū-'d-Dīn Mohammed, is left alone and is wishing to see me.

[1] This Saint, says Eflāki, was popularly known as Sirr-Dān, " The Confidant," a title signifying " one acquainted with secrets or mysteries."

I must go to the land of Rūm, and deliver over to
him the trust which my Teacher confided to my
safe keeping."

On arriving at Konieh, the Seyyid was so much
delighted with the discourse of Jelāl, that he kissed
the soles of his feet, exclaiming, " A hundred fold
hast thou surpassed thy father in all knowledge of
the Humanities ; but he was versed also in that
spiritual knowledge which is attained only through
silent contemplation and through ecstasy. From
this day forward my aim shall be to instruct thee in
that knowledge—the knowledge possessed by the
Prophets and Saints and which we term *The Science
of Divine Intuition*. This is the science spoken of
by Allah : ' We have taught him a science from
within Us.' [1] This knowledge did I acquire from
my Teacher ; do thou receive it from me, and thus
become the heir of thy father in things spiritual as
well as in things temporal." Jelāl took the Seyyid
to his College, and for nine years was his pupil in
mystic lore. [2]

The following story is told of Jelāl's student
days. While he was pursuing his studies at Aleppo,
the superior treatment he received from the professor roused the jealousy of some of his fellow
students, who complained to the governor that
Jelāl was immoral, as he was in the habit of quitting
his cell at midnight for some unknown purpose.
The governor resolved to see and judge for himself ;

[1] *Koran* xviii, 64.
[2] *Acts of the Adepts*, pp. 14-15.

he therefore hid himself in the college porter's lodge.

At midnight Jelāl came forth, and went straight to the locked gate of the college, watched by the governor. The gate flew open ; and Jelāl, followed at a distance by the governor, went through the streets to the locked city gate. This, too, opened of itself ; and again both passed through. They went on, and came to the tomb of Abraham (at Hebron, about 350 miles distant). There a domed edifice was seen, filled with a large company of forms in green raiment, who came forth to meet Jelāl, and conducted him into the building. The governor hereupon lost his senses through fright, and did not recover until after the sun had risen. He could now see neither edifice nor human being. He wandered about on a trackless waste for three days and nights, and at length sank under his sufferings.

Meanwhile the porter of the college had given intelligence of the governor's pursuit after Jelāl. When his officers found that he did not return, they sent a company of soldiers to seek him. These, on the second day, were met by Jelāl, who told them where they would find their master. Late on the next day they came up with the governor, found him nearly dead, and brought him home. This dignitary was so impressed by the event that he became a sincere admirer and devoted disciple of Jelāl. [1]

[1] *Acts of the Adepts*, p. 21.

The two following anecdotes also illustrate the faculty ascribed to the higher Mystics of transporting themselves at will to great distances.

A certain rich merchant of Konieh, a disciple, as was also his wife, of Jelál, went to Mekka one year for the pilgrimage. On the day when the victims are slaughtered,[1] the lady had a dish of sweetmeat prepared, and sent some of it in a china bowl to Jelál, to be eaten at dinner.[2] She made the request that, when he partook of the food, he would favour her absent husband with his remembrance, his prayers, and his blessing. Jelál invited his disciples to the feast, and all ate of the lady's sweetmeat to repletion. But the bowl still remained full. Jelál then said, " Oh, *he*, too, must partake of it." He took the bowl, ascended to the terraced roof of the college with it, returning immediately empty handed. His friends asked him what he had done with the bowl and the food. " I have handed them," said Jelál, " to the lady's husband, whose property they are." The company were puzzled by his words and conduct. In due course of time, when the pilgrims returned to Konieh, out of the baggage of the merchant the china bowl was produced, and sent in to the astonished lady, who enquired of her husband how he had become possessed of that identical dish. He replied, " Ah ! I am also at a loss to know how it happened. But on the eve of

---

[1] The *Qŭrban Bairam*, or annual sacrifice, which takes place while the pilgrims are at Mekka.

[2] This is a common custom in the East.

the slaughter of the victims, I was seated in my tent, at Arafāt, with a company of other pilgrims, when an arm was projected into the tent, and placed this dish before me, filled with sweetmeat. I sent out servants to see who had brought it to me, but no one was found." [1]

A company of pilgrims arrived one year at Konieh on the return journey from Mekka, and after visiting all the famous men of the city they were conducted to Jelāl's College. On seeing him seated there, they all exclaimed and fainted away. When they were recovered, Jelāl began to offer excuses, saying to them, " I fear you have been deceived, either by an imposter, or by some person resembling me in feature." The pilgrims, however, one and all objected. " Why talks he thus ? " they said to one another. " Why strive to make us doubt our eyes ? By the God of heaven and earth, he was with us in person, habited in the very dress he now wears, when we assumed the pilgrim garb at Mekka. He performed with us all the ceremonies of the pilgrimage there, and at Arafāt. He visited with us the tomb of the Prophet at Medina, though he never once ate or drank with us." [2]

For further examples of the marvellous acts of Jelālū-'d-Dīn as recorded by Eflāki, I must refer the curious reader to the work itself.

Perhaps the most famous among the Saints of the Turkish Conquest was Hadji Bektāsh—" Bektāsh the Pilgrim "—before mentioned. He was a man

---

[1] *Acts of the Adepts*, p. 62.   [2] *Ibid.*, p. 60.

of noble birth and great learning, his father having been the Seyyid Ibrahim Mokerrem of Khorassan. While yet a boy, he is said to have been distinguished for his devotion, never mixing with companions of his own age ; and evinced in early youth an aversion to all worldly pursuits. His education was entrusted to the Sage, Lokmān, one of the disciples of Achmet Youssouf, the Chief of the Sheikhs of Turkestan, and by him Hadji Bektāsh was " instructed in all the exoteric and esoteric sciences." Lokmān bestowed on this favourite pupil the mantle of the Imām Jafer, which he had himself received from Achmet Youssouf. According to his biographers, Hadji Bektāsh declined all the dignities offered him by his father, " who died a prince in Khorassan," and devoted himself to a life of seclusion. Forty years were passed by this saintly man in study, fasting, and prayer, until he at length arrived at such a degree of perfection that his soul during sleep, left his body and entered the World of Spirits, and he became " filled with Mystic Science and Divine Knowledge." In obedience to the spiritually received command of Achmet Youssouf he went with Mohammed Bokhara and seven hundred Dervishes and other pious men and saints into Asia Minor in the train of the conquering Orchan.

It appears to be a point of honour with a Dervish to maintain that the Order of which he is a member is the most important of all the religious sects of Islam, and that its Founder is the greatest and holiest of all *Pirs*. The legends related of Hadji Bektāsh by his followers, however, go far to establish his supremacy over all rival Saints. Of these the following may serve as a specimen.

Hadji Bektāsh was one day sitting with some of his followers on a wall, when they saw a rival Dervish advancing towards them, mounted on a roaring lion, and holding in his hand as a whip, a writhing serpent with which he chastised his steed. The disciples, who had never before beheld such a sight, marvelled greatly ; but their Sheikh calmly observed, " My brethren, there is little merit in being able to ride upon a lion ; I will show you a more wonderful thing. This wall on which we are sitting shall advance and bar the further progress of yon wild beast and his rider." The Dervishes immediately found that they were being carried forward by the wall towards the lion, whose rider was compelled to acknowledge the superior spiritual rank of Hadji Bektāsh. Evliyā Effendi relates in his " Travels " that this wall, which was still in his day of large proportions, and even the identical spot on which the Saint was seated when he performed the miracle, was pointed out to him at Sari-beg in Asia Minor.

Michelet has remarked, with reference to the legends which have collected round the Saints of the Christian Calendar, that " the monks wrote them, but the people were their authors." [1] And

---

[1] " Les Moines les écrivirent, mais le peuple les faisait." *La Sorcière*, p. 15.

the same may be said of most of the extravagant stories related of Dervish Saints. In the following story, for instance, the Moslem Saint, Mohammed Bokhara, is made the hero of adventures evidently borrowed from a widespread Eastern folktale.

This Mohammed Bokhara, also called Sari Saltik and Kilgra Sultan, was one of the fighting saints of the Ottoman conquest, and a favourite disciple of Hadji Bektāsh. After the conquest of Broussa by Sultan Orchan (1326), the Master bestowed on his disciple the insignia of the Order—a wooden sword, a sheepskin mat, a banner, drum, and horn— and despatched him on a mission to the Unbelievers. The Saint and his seventy followers spread their sheepskins on the sea and sailed away, " with drums beating and banners flying, from Roumelia to the Crimea, from Muscovy to Poland." At Dantzic, Sari Saltik had an interview with Saint Nikola the Patriarch, whom he slew. Then, adopting his name and dress, he, as the Patriarch, travelled about Europe for some years, during which time he converted many thousands to the faith of Islam. The King of the Dobrudja, after listening to the preaching of the Saint, desired of him a miracle in confirmation of his mission. There happened to be then in the Dobrudja a terrible seven-headed Dragon, and the King's two daughters were doomed to be devoured by him. Sari Saltik agreed to slay the monster and deliver the princesses on condition that they became Moslems.

Accompanied by his seventy Dervishes, beating

their drums and waving their banners, he proceeded to the column to which the doomed maidens were bound, drew his wooden sword, and waited. The Dragon soon appeared, and the Saint, addressing him with the passage from the Koran beginning " Greetings to Noah in Both Worlds," cut off three of his heads so that he fled away with the remaining four. The Dervish pursued him to his den, at the entrance to which he cut off the remaining heads, and then followed the monster into the cave, where a frightful struggle took place. The Dragon pressed the Saint so hard against the rock that the impression of his hands and feet remained visible. At last Sari Saltik slew the monster, and, with his bloody breast and bloody sword, he led the maidens back to their father, the king.

In the meantime, however, a " cursed (Christian) monk" who had shown Saltik the way to the column, had picked up the three tongues and the ears of the three heads first cut off and carried them to the king, boasting that he had killed the Dragon. The princesses bore out the testimony of the Saint ; but the monk persisting in his statement, Sari Saltik proposed as a test that they should be both broiled together in a cauldron. The monk did not approve of this trial by ordeal ; but, by command of the King, he was obliged to undergo it. Sari Saltik was tied up by his Dervishes, and the monk by his companions, and both were put into a large cauldron heated by an immense fire. It was at this hour that Hadji Bektāsh, who was then at

Kir Shehir in Asia Minor, swept with a handkerchief a dripping rock, exclaiming, " My Saltik Mohammed is now in great distress, may Allah assist him ! " Ever since that day, salt, instead of, as before, fresh water, has dripped from that rock, and from it the kind of salt called " Hadji Bektāsh " is produced. The cauldron being opened, Sari Saltik was found perspiring and ejaculating " O All Vivifying ! (*Yā Hayī*);[1] but of the monk nothing was left but blackened cinders and burnt bones. The King of the Dobrudja, moved by this miracle, instantly, together with seven thousand of his subjects, embraced the faith of Islam. He also sent ambassadors to Sultan Orchan, who bestowed upon him the title of *Kadi*, a horse-tail standard, a banner, and the Moslem name of Ali Mukhtar.

In the same year Sari Saltik made his will, wherein he commanded seven coffins to be made, because seven Kings were to contend for his body after death. And so it fell out. After his corpse had been washed and laid in one of the coffins, seven kings demanded the privilege of burying it. A coffin was given to all the seven, who were " the Kings of Muscovy, Poland, Bohemia, Sweden, Adrianople, Moldavia, and the Dobrudja." The last buried the coffin that fell to him in the Cave of the Dragon at Kilgra on the Black Sea, and built a Tekkéh close by, where the Saint's wooden sword, drum, and banner were treasured as relics.[2]

[1] One of the attributes of the Deity
[2] *Narrative of Travels.*

Of the many Dervish saints whose *turbés* or
mausoleums are to be found in that picturesque
old capital of the Ottoman Sultans, Broussa, one
of the most famous was Shemsū-'d-Dīn Mohammed
Ben Ali, a Seyyid, or descendant of the Prophet,
who also bore the honourable title of Emir Sultan, [1]
bestowed on him on account of his learning. When
performing his pilgrimage to the holy cities, the
Sherifs, his fellow descendants, refused him the
portion to which he was entitled by his descent.
The Saint accordingly decided to refer the matter
to the decision of the Prophet himself, and, going
to his tomb accompanied by the other Seyyids,
they heard a voice from within cry " Health to
thee, my son Mohammed Ben Ali ! go to Rūm [2]
with the lamp ! " Upon hearing this, the Sherifs
threw themselves at Shemsū-'d-Dīn's feet, and
acknowledged their fault. He shortly afterwards
set out for Anatolia, whereupon a lamp suspended
from heaven became his guide on the way, and
disappeared only when he entered the gates of
Broussa. Emir Sultan accepted this as a sign that
he was to take up his abode in this city, where he
found awaiting him four hundred thousand disciples. [3] For the inhabitants had seen the lamp
hanging from heaven for three days, and knew by
that wonder that they might expect the advent of a

[1] Referred to on p. 33.   [2] See note, p. 16.
[3] This is evidently one of the characteristically Oriental
exaggerations with which Evliya Effendi is frequently
taxed by his translator.

Saint. Under his direction they all became Dervishes. Sultan Bayazid not only walked on foot
by his stirrup, but gave him his daughter Nutüfer
Hanŭm in marriage. When this Sultan had completed the building of the Oulou Jāmi,[1] or " Great
Mosque," he asked Emir Sultan if it were not
a perfect mosque. " Yes," replied the Saint, " it
is a very elegant mosque, but some cups of wine
for the refreshment of the pious are wanting in the
middle." The Sultan exclaimed with surprise,
" How would it be possible to stain the house of
Allah with the liquor forbidden by the law ? "
" Well," replied the Saint, " thou hast built a
mosque, Bayazid, and findest it strange to put a
cup of wine therein ; but thy body, which is a
house of Allah more excellent than a talisman
composed of the Divine Names, or the throne of
Allah Himself—how is it that thou dost not fear
to stain the purity of *this* godlike house with wine,
day and night ? " From that moment, adds the
narrator, " Bayazid repented, and left off drinking
wine."

Among the number of holy men who favoured
Evliya Effendi with their friendship, was the Sheikh
Abdi Dédéh, who built the Mevlevi Monastery at
Kassim Pasha, on the outskirts of the capital.

[1] Three Sultans took part in the building of this magnificent mosque, Murad I, Bayazid I, and Mohammed I. The
interior is divided by pillars into twenty-five halls, each
roofed with a separate dome. It is, however, not this
" Great Mosque," but another that bears the name of
" Bayazid Ilderim."

According to this author, Sheikh Abdi was "in mystic lore, a second Jelālū-'d-Dīn. He knew by their names all those who came to the convent, though he had never seen them before. When he sang, "he intoxicated all Dervishes." Evliya Effendi also narrates that, as Sultan Murad was on one occasion returning from Broussa to Constantinople by sea, he was in danger of being drowned near Cape Bozbournou, when he "saw at the ship's head the Sheikh, who calmed the waves."

Of the Saints canonized in our own days I may mention a Sheikh of Cavalla, whose gift of prophecy had enabled him to predict the day and hour of his departure from the world. This holy man caused his tomb to be prepared in the hall of the *Tekkeh*; and, though apparently in his usual health, he, on the eve of the appointed day, announced to his wife and his disciples that he must now take leave of them, as that day would be his last. These farewells taken, he calmly proceeded alone to the hall and lay down in the tomb that was to be his last resting-place. When, on the following morning, the disciples arrived at the *Tekkeh*, they found that their revered master had indeed, according to his prediction, breathed his last. The fame of his holy life and the circumstances of his death soon became widely known in the neighbourhood; the devout watchers did not fail to see supernatural lights hovering over his grave; and before long miracles of healing were reported to have been performed at the shrine of the Sheikh of Cavalla.

CHAPTER XI

WOMEN MYSTICS

" Her Woman's sex dims not the Sun's effulgent ray ;
Though Masculine the Moon, he lighteth not the day." [1]
From the Arabic.

IT is characteristic of the high estimation in which
women have always been held by the Sūfis that the
place of honour among the early mystics is by them
assigned to a woman. This distinguished person was
Rābia al Adawia, also called *Umm al Khair* (" The
Mother of Good,") a native of Bássora, who lived
in the eighth century, and whose reputed grave on
Mount Tor, to the east of Jerusalem, became, like
those of the generality of Moslem saints, a place of
pilgrimage. The words and actions of this Queen
of Mystics have been recorded by many Oriental
writers, [2] and contain a germ of Sūfism, or kind of
sentimental pantheism, which often found poetical
or rhythmic expression. An eminent Sūfi writer
of the twelfth century, Ibn Khamis Al Juhani,
relates in his works many anecdotes of Rābia's
sanctity and piety, some of which are quoted by
Ibn Khallikan in his *Biographical Dictionary*. The
following verse is attributed to her :—

My heart I keep for Thy communion, Lord !
And those who seek me but my body find.
My guests may with my body converse hold,
But my Belov'd alone holds converse with my heart.

[1] In Arabic, as in German, the Moon is masculine and the
Sun feminine.
[2] M. Dozy, however, attaches no historical value to the
legends concerning Rābia. *Essai, etc.*, p. 318-19.

It is related that on one occasion the celebrated
Moslem theologians, Hassan of Bássora and Shākik
of Balk, came to visit this pious lady when she was
ill. The former greeted her in mystic fashion with
the following couplet :—

> He in his faith cannot be all sincere,
> Who mourns the chastening of his Master dear.

Shākik added, correcting his friend:—

> He in his faith cannot be all sincere,
> Who joys not, chastened by his Master dear.

Rābia's enthusiasm, however, went beyond that of
her eminent and reverend guests, and she replied :—

> He in his faith cannot be all sincere,
> Who *feels* a smart when draws his Master near !

Another eminent contemporary theologian,
Sofyan ath Thauri, exclaimed one day in her
presence, "O what anguish is mine!" Rābia
reproved him, saying, "Speak not a lie, but rather
say, 'O how little anguish is mine!' If thou wert
really in affliction thou couldst not sigh." One
of the Sūfi brethren relates that in his prayers he
was accustomed to invoke Rābia, who appeared to
him in a vision, and said : "Thy offerings were
presented to us on trays of light, and covered with
napkins of light." She often said, "If my good
works appear to the world, I count them as
nought," and one of her counsels was : "Hide thy
good deeds as thou wouldst hide thy sins." One of
her biographers gives a story as related by Abda, a
handmaid of this pious lady : "Rābia used to pass
the whole night in prayer, and at morning dawn

she took a short sleep in her oratory till daylight ; and I have heard her exclaim, springing from her couch as if in dread : 'O my soul ! how long wilt thou sleep ? When wilt thou awake ? Soon thou shalt sleep to rise no more till the call shall summon thee on the Day of Resurrection ! ' This was her constant custom till the day of her death. On its approach, she called me and said, 'O Abda ! inform none of my death, and shroud me in this gown.' This was a gown of hair-cloth which she wore when praying at the time when the eyes of others were closed in sleep. I shrouded her in that gown and in a woollen veil which she used to wear ; and about a year afterwards I saw her in a dream, clothed in a gown and veil of green silk, the like of which for beauty I never beheld. And I said, 'O Rābia ! what has become of the gown in which I shrouded thee, and of the woollen veil ? ' To which she answered, 'By Allah ! it was taken off me, and I received in exchange what thou seest on me ; my shroud was folded up, a seal was put upon it, and it was taken up to the highest heaven, that by it my reward might be complete on the day of resurrection.' 'It was for this,' I observed, 'that thou didst work when in the world.' 'And what is this,' she rejoined, 'compared with what I have seen of Allah's bounty to his Saints ? ' I asked her in what state was Obaida (a holy woman who had predeceased her), and she replied, 'It cannot be described. By Allah ! She has surpassed us all, and reached the highest place in Paradise.'

'And how is that,' said I, 'when all men considered thee far, far above her?' 'Because,' she replied, 'when in the world she took no thought for the morrow, nor even for the coming night.'"

In the *Acts of the Adepts*, and elsewhere, we also find records of many holy women, some of whom were honoured with the friendship of the poet-saint Jelālū-'d-Dīn; and not least eminent among them were his wife, Kīrā Khātŭn, and his daughter-in-law, Fātimā. The latter had been taught to read and write by Jelāl, who bestowed upon her the complimentary title of his "Right Eye"; her sister he called his "Left Eye"; and their mother, Lātifā Khātŭn, "the Personification of God's grace." "Fātimā," says the story, "was a Saint, and continually worked miracles. She fasted by day, and watched by night, tasting food only once in three days. She was very charitable to the poor, the orphans, and the widows, distributing to them food and raiment."

Kīrā Khātŭn was also a most saintly woman. She was Jelālū-'d-Dīn's second wife, and survived him. When she, too, departed this life, and was about to be buried by the side of her husband, a strange incident occurred. As her corpse was being borne towards its last resting-place, the procession passed through one of the gates of the town (Konieh). Here the bearers found themselves arrested by some unseen power, so that they could not move hand or foot. This singular effect lasted for about half an hour. Her stepson, Sultan Veled, struck up a hymn and commenced a holy dance, after which the bearers recovered the use of their limbs and the interment was completed. That same night a holy man of the fraternity saw Kīrā Khātŭn in heaven by the side of her husband, and enquired of her the reason of the arrestation of the funeral. She informed him thus :—

" On the previous day a man and a woman had on that spot, been stoned to death for adultery. I took compassion on them, interceded for their forgiveness, and obtained for them admission to Paradise. My preoccupation on their behalf was the reason of the delay met with by the funeral procession." [1]

According to Eflāki, there lived at Konieh in the days of Jelālū-'d-Dīn, a saintly lady named Fakhrū-'n-Nisā (" The Glory of Women "), who enjoyed the acquaintance of the holy men of the time,

[1] *The Mesnevi*, p. 119. This curious legend appears to illustrate the Moslem notion that the soul remains with the body until after burial, and that it is only then—except, perhaps, in the case of such saintly persons as Kīrā Khātŭn —that its ultimate destiny is decided. After the last rites have been performed by the relatives, the Imām is left alone by the grave in order, it is said, to prompt the deceased in his replies to the " Questioners." These are the two Angels, Mounkir and Nekir, who, according to Moslem belief, enter the grave with the dead in order to interrogate them concerning their faith. If the dead has been a devout Moslem, his reply will be " My God is Allah ; my Prophet, Mohammed ; my religion, Islam ; and my *Kibla*, the Ka'aba." If, however, he has been but an indifferent follower of the Prophet, he will not be able to remember this formula.

all of whom were aware of her sanctity. Miracles were wrought by her in countless numbers. She constantly attended the meetings at Jelāl's house and received occasionally visits from him. Her friends suggested that she ought to go and perform the pilgrimage to Mekka ; but she would not decide upon so serious an undertaking without first consulting Jelāl. Accordingly, she went to see him. As she entered his presence, before she spoke, he called out to her : "Oh most happy idea ! May thy journey be prosperous ! God willing, we shall be together." She bowed, but said nothing. The disciples present were puzzled. "That night she remained a guest at Jelāl's house, conversing with him till past midnight, when, according to his custom, he went to perform his devotions on the housetop. Presently he called to her to come up also, and when she did so, she saw the holy Ka'aba of Mekka revolving in the air above the head of Jelāl. So overcome was Fakhrū-'n-Nisā by this wondrous sight, that she sank down in a swoon. On recovering she came to the conclusion that it was not necessary for her to undertake the difficult and dangerous journey to the Holy City, as its chief attraction had been thus marvellously revealed to her."

In later centuries also it would appear that Societies of pious women have been from time to time affiliated with the Dervish Orders. These holy women are frequently mentioned in the biographies of Dervish Saints, either individually, or collectively by some such name as " The Sisters of Rūm," alluded to in the writings of Hadji Bektāsh. Nor is such mystical devotion entirely unknown among Osmanli women at the present day. The widow of the Cavalla Sheikh above referred to, a woman of great intelligence, presided, after her husband's death, over a society of female devotees who held their meetings at her residence. A British subject who had had business relations with the Sheikh in connection with the tobacco-growing industry of Cavalla and the neighbourhood, from which the revenues of the *Tekkeh* were derived, obtained from this lady many curious details concerning her Sisterhood, and was even allowed by her to be a hidden spectator of their devotions. During the first years of my residence at Salonica I chanced to come into contact with a Turkish lady who was always referred to as " the Dervish Hanŭm," and enjoyed the reputation of being no mean poetess. Though sufficiently liberal minded to admit European ladies to her acquaintance and visit them in their own houses, she, however, always skilfully parried any attempt to elicit information with respect to the Sisterhood of Mystics of which report proclaimed her to be a distinguished member.

In the earlier times of Islam much greater freedom of manners appears to have existed than has been the case in later centuries. Indeed the records of the Prophet's commands on the subject of the seclusion of women, and the glimpses we have in the Koran and in the writings of the Commentators

of the social life of his time, do not point to any
greater " subjection of women " than that enjoined
by the Apostle Paul ; and the women of the Prophet's
household evidently held a much higher position,
and were treated with far more respect than are the
women of a provincial Armenian family at the present day. The Turkish harem system, though less
rigid than is generally believed in Europe, naturally
offers great obstacles to the formation of sister-
hoods. And the natural result of denying to women
any social intercourse with the other sex has been
to stifle any desire for even that moderate amount
of education necessary to enable them to read and
appreciate the spiritual writings by which their
husbands and brothers are influenced. For though
it is naturally the more ignorant among Moslem
women who believe most implicitly in the wonder-
working powers of Dervish Sheikhs, it is on the
other hand only women who have received a good
Turkish education who " enter on the Mystic Path,"
and are distinguished by the title of *Sūfi Hanŭm*.

CHAPTER XII

"Not at Strife's door sits he ; when thwarted ne'er
Starts up to contest ; all unmoved his soul,
He is no Saint who from the Path would stir
Though a huge rock should from a mountain roll."

AFTER the establishment of the twelve original
Orders, the numbers of the Dervishes greatly increased in all the Asiatic countries which had come
under the influence of Islam. In the train of Ala-
'd-Dīn, Sultan of Iconium, and his successor Orchan,
they spread themselves over Asia Minor ; and,
after the conquest of Broussa by the latter prince,
the munificence of the victors, who attributed the
success of their armies to the presence of these holy
men, enabled the Dervish Sheikhs to found monasteries and colleges in all parts of the Empire. For
the Founders, at least, of these early Orders were, as
has been seen, men of great learning and wide
culture, as well as of saintly life.

The slopes of the Bithynian Olympus rising
steeply behind the ancient Ottoman capital of
Broussa, which had for centuries previously been
the resort of Christian hermits and cenobites, were
now taken possession of by Moslem recluses who here
established themselves among the flocks of the
Turcoman nomads ; and the coolness and quiet of
the retreats which had favoured the holy idleness of

Christian monks, now charmed the reveries of
Dervish poets and the meditations of Sūfi philosophers. Their honoured tombs may still be seen at
the foot of the mountain where they passed their
lives, or in the vicinity of the Schools of Philosophy
in which they taught. Amid these beautiful and
romantic surroundings, after having themselves drunk
deeply of the wells of science, they spread their senti-
ments, their ideas, and their knowledge in works which
will live as long as the Ottoman language and nation
endure. Sultan Orchan, who acknowledged that he
had conquered Broussa by their spiritual aid, placed
the most distinguished among the Sheikhs at the
head of the Schools he founded, endowed them
with liberal salaries, and honoured them with
complimentary titles.

The influence exercised by the Dervishes over the
minds of the people generally, though often, as we
have seen, made use of by the Sultans and their
Ministers for State purposes, has occasionally caused
alarm, and the Orders have in consequence not
only been at such times regarded with suspicion, but
subjected to active persecution. The earliest, and
in fact, the general, accusation brought against these
mystics was that their practices were contrary to the
spirit of Islam and the express commands of the Prophet ; and from the time of their first formation,
under the Khalifs, attempts were made to stop the
progress of this enthusiasm for a monastic life. In
these attempts the civil power had the entire concur-
rence of the *Ulema* or Legists who, as students and

expounders of the Koranic Law, found their own spiritual supremacy menaced, and were naturally jealous of the growing influence and importance of this rival sect. Under the pretence of defending Moslem orthodoxy, but in reality to maintain their own power and prestige, they became the formidable auxiliaries of the government in a struggle which menaced at one time the throne itself.[1] But the active opposition to the Dervishes appears always to have been rather spasmodic and intermittent than regular and systematic ; and what ground they lost at one period and under one sovereign they often more than regained under his successor.

In the nineteenth century, as in the days of Orchan, their influence has been made use of by Sultans and Generals to excite the zeal and courage of their troops in battle. Whenever a military campaign had been organised, a number of Dervishes from nearly all the Orders hasten to join the army. Commanding officers gladly engage their services and treat them with every respect and consideration, as their presence in the camp, where they spend whole days and nights fasting in their tents, while offering supplications and making vows for the success of the arms of the True Believers, maintains a most desirable religious enthusiasm among the troops. On the eve of an action the Dervishes roam excitedly through the camp, rehearsing the benefits promised by the Prophet to all who fight for the Faith of Islam, or who die in

[1] Ubicini, *Lettres sur la Turquie*, Vol. I, p. 166.

arms, and seek to rouse the zeal and animate the courage of the soldiers by every means in their power. During a battle their excitement increases, and their voices may be heard above the din of war, shouting, " O Victors ! " (*Yā Ghazi*) ; " O Martyrs ! " (*Yā Shahid*) ; " *Yā Allah* ! " or *Yā Hoo !* " (O Him). If they fancy the Holy Standard, the mantle of the Prophet, to be in danger, they crowd round the sacred relic to strengthen the lines of the officers stationed as its guard, and not only sustain their efforts, but themselves perform prodigies of valour. A Dervish of high renown in his day, Ak Shemsū-'d'Din by name, is said to have foretold to Mohammed "the Conqueror" the day and hour of the fall of Constantinople. Together with seventy-seven other " distinguished and holy men beloved of Allah," he accompanied the Sultan to that memorable siege ; and the Sultan made a covenant with them that one half of the city should belong to them and the other half to the Moslem conquerors. " And I will," said he, " build for each of you a monastery, an almshouse, a college, and a School of Sacred Traditions (*Dar-'l-Hadis*)." The deeds of valour achieved by these enthusiasts at the taking of Constantinople, and the miracles performed in answer to their prayers are recorded—and, it need hardly be said, exaggerated—by Moslem historians ; and the tombs of many are to this day places of pilgrimage for the Faithful.

Nor were the Dervishes held in less honour by succeeding Sultans. After the capture of the

Byzantine capital and the consolidation of the Empire, their poets and writers remained in high favour at Court, and there were few Padishahs who were not enrolled as members of one or more of the Orders. The long reign of Bayazid II (1481–1521) also bears traces of the influence of Mystic philosophy on the Court. The most renowned Dervish of that time, the Sheikh Jasi, had, when about to start on a pilgrimage to Mekka, foretold to Bayazid, then governor of Amasia, that on his return from the Holy City he would find the Prince on the throne, and it fell out as he had predicted. This eminent man received the titles of " Sheikh of Sultans," and " Sultan of Sheikhs," and his cell was the meeting-place of all the dignitaries of the Empire. The Turkish writers Seadeddin and Ali narrate the biographies of thirty eminent Dervishes who flourished in the reign of this Sultan, called by many Ottoman historians " Bajazid the Sūfi." The influence of the Dervish society by which this Sultan surrounded himself may also be seen in his poetry, which breathes a spirit of mysticism and philosophy markedly absent from the writings of his talented but unhappy brother, Prince Djem, and his son, Selim I.

Notwithstanding the secular hostility of the Ulema, it does not appear that, previous to the 16th century, the Dervish Orders were interfered with by the Government. For so long as the substance of the doctrines held by the higher grades of these mystics was kept secret, the denunciations by the Legists of their ascetic practices, their vows, the dancing and other peculiar exercises performed in their *Tekkehs*, their pretensions to miraculous gifts, and claims to direct communion with the Deity, had but little effect. But as the influence and prestige of the Dervishes increased, many of the Orders relaxed by degrees the prudence and severity of their original rules, and allowed much of their doctrine to become publicly known. Their enemies were now enabled to make definite and serious charges against them. They were accused of attempting to make innovations on the dogmas of Islam ; of following practices forbidden by the Koran ; of denying the very existence of a personal Allah ; of teaching disrespect for all established institutions ; and of setting at nought all law, both human and divine. Their religious exercises were denounced as profane acts ; and it was asserted that all kinds of abominable practices were indulged in by them in the seclusion of their monasteries. The general tendency of the Dervish institutions appeared to the Ulema to threaten also the introduction into Islam of something analogous to the " Holy Priesthood " and " Apostolic Succession " of the Romish Church—ideas utterly at variance with the spirit of the Koran. An alleged discovery that gave a still greater shock to the orthodox mind was that the Dervishes concluded some of their prayers by anathematising the Ommiade Khalifs and glorifying the Khalif Ali ; and, consequently, that, though nominally *Sūnnis*, they virtually belonged to the heterodox sect of the *Shiās*.

There seems, however, little reason to doubt that whenever overt hostility has been manifested against the Dervish Orders by a Sultan and his Ministers it has invariably been prompted by political, rather than religious motives. For notwithstanding the odium cast upon these Mystics by the Legists, no active measures, as above remarked, appear to have been taken against them by the Government until the beginning of the sixteenth century, when political events caused them to be looked upon as a possible source of danger to the State.

A new dynasty had been founded in Persia at this period on the basis of religion. The Sūfi Philosophy had always been popular in that country ; and Persia was at the same time the stronghold of the Shiā heresy and of the Dervish Fraternities. A Dervish Sheikh, named Eidar, who traced his descent from the Khalif Ali, having gained a great reputation for sanctity and a numerous following of disciples and adherents, assumed the title of " Sūfi" *par excellence*, and declared himself to have been commissioned by Allah to work a religious reformation. Sheikh Eidar perished in the attempt ; but his young son, Ismaïl, was protected by his faithful disciples, who took refuge with him in Ghilān, and carefully trained him in his father's principles. In 1501, at the head of a numerous body of partisans, Ismaïl revived the claims of Sheikh Eidar ; and, gradually overcoming all opposition, he at length became the founder of the Sūfi Dynasty, and the ruler of an extensive Empire.

His doctrines gained also many adherents in the Asiatic provinces of the Ottoman Empire, where Selim I took early and vigorous measures to suppress this new heretical sect. For, as Church and State are, in Islam, identical, a blow aimed at the one menaces equally the other ; and the great schism of the *Sūnnis* and *Shiās* is not a mere diversity of opinion purely religious and theoretic, but also a practical political dispute concerning the succession to the Khalifate, the headship of the Moslem Faith. Sultan Selim, whose inquisitorial talents are celebrated by Ottoman historians, organised a system of secret police by means of which he caused to be made out a list of all his subjects belonging to the Sūfi sect. Their number amounted to seventy thousand, forty thousand of whom were massacred, the rest being imprisoned for life. In Damascus a few hours sufficed for the extermination of the whole community of schismatic Mahommedans. The Persian monarch shortly afterwards declared war against the destroyer of his co-religionists, and a sanguinary campaign ensued. The Ottoman Dervishes in European Turkey, whose *Shiā* tendencies were more than suspected, were, very naturally, looked upon with disfavour during the course of these events, the Ulema making the most of this favourable opportunity by exciting the minds of the populace as well as of the authorities against their rivals.

A new sect, created about the beginning of the sixteenth century by Sheikh Hamza and called after him the Hamzavis, appears to have been, from its very foundation, in bad repute with the orthodox; and Sheikh Hamza was arrested and subsequently executed by order of the Sheikh-ul-Islam, the ostensible charge against him being that he omitted to repeat at his devotions the obligatory number of the *Isma i Sherif*, or "Praises of the Prophet." By the rest of the Dervishes he was naturally regarded as a martyr, and his reputation for piety and extraordinary powers still survives in the capital. Another Sheikh of the same Order was also put to death shortly afterwards on an accusation of heterodoxy, together with forty of his disciples, who appear to have voluntarily given themselves up to the authorities. And so great was the effervescence of the orthodox under several succeeding reigns, and particularly in that of Mohammed IV, that the Ulema and other rigid Mohammedans even ventured to propose the extermination of all the Orders, the confiscation of their revenues, and the destruction of their monasteries. An attempt was, indeed, made by the Grand Vizier of that Sultan, Achmet Kiupruli, to suppress the Bektāshi, Khālvetti, Djelvetti, and Shemshi Orders. Like all former and subsequent attempts, however, it succeeded but partially, as the Government was overawed by the Janisseries, whose intimate connection with the Bektāshi Order made them the allies of the Dervishes generally, and the Porte feared to do anything that might arouse the resentment of this formidable force.

The action of the Sultans, too, seems to have been but half-hearted; for it is recorded that even Selim I,—whom Mouradjā D'Ohsson describes as "poet, parricide and fratricide, mystic, tyrant, and conqueror,"[1]—made pilgrimages to the tombs of deceased, and to the cells of living Sheikhs of repute ; and that he raised at Damascus a mosque over the grave of the eminent saint, Muhajjin el Arābi. Suleyman I also built at Konieh, in honour of Jelālū-'d-Dīn, a mosque, a *Tekkeh*, and public alms-kitchen. At Sidi Ghazi he erected a great establishment with a *Tekkeh* and college for the Bektāshis, and he also repaired the *Tekkeh* covering the tomb of Abdūl Kādr Ghilāni, the sainted founder of the Kādiri Order, thus drawing upon himself the benedictions of three influential Orders.

After this stormy period the Orders appear to have enjoyed a long interval of freedom from persecution. For Evliya Effendi, writing towards the end of the seventeenth century, makes no mention of the existence of any popular ill-feeling towards the Dervishes with whom he was closely connected during the whole of his long and adventurous life. The massacre of the Janisseries by Mahmoud II, the " Reformer," in the beginning of last century, was, however, followed by persecution of the Bektāshi Order, who were suspected of having been concerned in the revolts that ensued. Its members were accused of treason against the State, and the chief Legists agreed with the Sultan that a severe

[1] *Histoire de l'Empire Ottomane*, Part I, p. 377.

sentence should be passed upon the Brotherhood.
Its three principal Sheikhs were consequently publicly executed ; the Order was declared abolished,
many of its *Tekkehs* were destroyed, and its members generally were banished from the capital,
those who remained being compelled to abandon
their distinctive dress.[1]

This determined action on the part of the Government spread consternation throughout the Dervish
Orders in the Empire, whose members feared for the
moment that they, like the Bektāshis, were all
doomed to destruction or dispersion ; and, to use
the expressive Oriental phrase, " They remained
motionless, expecting their last day, devoured by
anguish, and with their backs resting against the
wall of stupefaction." But here Sultan Mahmoud
paused in his work of destruction. " Though "—to
use the metaphors of the historian of the massacre
of the Janisseries—" he had not feared to open
with the sword a road for public happiness by
cutting down the thorny bushes that obstructed
his progress and tore his imperial mantle," he
hesitated to decree the entire destruction of institutions which had enjoyed the respect and devotion
of his predecessors and of Moslems generally for
upwards of a thousand years.[2] This " hesitation,"
is, however, not so surprising when we learn the

[1] Ubicini, *Lettres sur la Turquie*, Vol. I, p. 107.

[2] Ubicini, who stigmatises the doctrines of the Sūfis as
" abominable," appears to regret that the Dervishes were
not then destroyed root and branch. See his *Lettres*, etc.,
Vol. I, pp. 101 and 114-115.

fact, of which Ubicini appears to have been ignorant, that Sultan Mahmoud was an affiliated member of the Mevlevi *Tekkeh* at Pera, and frequently visited it ; and that he also honoured with his presence the meetings of a Nakshibendi fraternity established in the suburb of Foundoukli.[1]

The Dervishes, however, on finding that the blow dealt at the Bektāshis was not followed by the suppression or even persecution of the other Orders, soon recovered from their consternation ; and the more fanatical among them set on foot a secret agitation with the object of inciting the populace against a Sultan who had dared to raise his hand against " the chosen of Allah." In 1837 Mahmoud narrowly escaped falling a victim to the frenzied zeal of one of these ascetics. As he was crossing the Bridge of Galata, surrounded by his escort, a long-haired cenobite, commonly known in the capital as " The Hairy Sheikh," darted from among the bystanders, and, seizing the bridle of the Sultan's horse, exclaimed, " *Giaour Padishah !* (Infidel Sultan !) Art thou not yet satiated with abominations ? Thou shalt answer to Allah for thy impieties. Thou destroyest the institutions of thy Brethren ; thou ruinest Islam, and drawest down the wrath of Allah on thyself and on the nation ! " The Sultan, fearing that popular feeling might be roused against himself by the ascetic's denunciations, commanded his guards to remove the madman from his path. " Madman ! " echoed the infuriated Dervish.

[1] John Brown, *The Dervishes*, p. 346-347 n.

"Sayest thou that I am mad? The spirit of Allah, which inspires me, and which I must obey, has commanded me to declare His truth, and promised me the reward of the Faithful!" The fanatic was, however, seized and put to death without delay. His body was given up to his brethren, who buried it with the honours due to a martyr; and on the following day a report was circulated that the watchers had seen a *Nūr*, or supernatural light, hovering over the grave of the Sheikh—a convincing proof of the favour with which Allah had regarded his action.

It needed, however, a bold reformer to put a noisy fanatic to death, and the majority of Sultans and statesmen have contented themselves with exiling to some remote part of the Empire a Dervish whose influence on the populace they had cause to fear.

Generally speaking, whenever public hostility has been excited against the Dervish Orders it has had its foundation in the horror with which the orthodox *Sunni* Mohammedans regard the *Shiā* heresy, and this hostility seems never to have been very general or of long continuance. For those whose religious principles and devotion to the purity of the creed of Islam incited them to combat the growing power of the Dervishes, have invariably been, in their turn, combated by other principles drawn from the same source; the majority of the Turkish nation having always regarded the Dervishes, their Sheikhs, and, above all, the Founders of the Orders, as the beloved Sons of Heaven, and in intimate relations with spiritual powers. These opinions have for basis the tradition that the different Orders originated, as above mentioned, in the two congregations of Abū Bekr and Ali, and that the grace bestowed upon them by the Prophet, both as his relations and Vicars, had been miraculously transmitted through the series of Sheikhs who, from age to age, have governed the monastic societies. It is also popularly believed that the legion of Saints, constituting the Mohammedan spiritual hierarchy alluded to in a previous chapter as perpetually existing among mankind, are to be found among the members of the Dervish fraternities. Consequently, to condemn, persecute, and destroy them, as was the unanimous cry of the Legists, would have been to draw upon the whole nation the wrath of all the holy Saints. Even the less enthusiastic did not dare openly to declare themselves hostile to the Dervishes. Moslems generally respect what is beyond their comprehension, and hold this mixture of religious practices and profane exercises to be a mystery which the True Believer should treat with silent and unquestioning reverence. And the superstitious ideas which these ascetics have the talent to perpetuate in their nation have always served as their shield. So persistent, too, is the influence of, and veneration for, the spiritual character of the more eminent among the Sheikhs, that even those Ottomans whose education and intercourse with Europeans might be supposed to have freed them from national superstition, are often found to be still under the influence of the ideas inculcated in youth. This is forcibly illustrated by an incident which was related to me during my sojourn at Salonica.

A Pasha, who had represented his Government at Paris, and whose sprightly wit, liberal ideas, and pleasant manners had, in his younger days, rendered him a great favourite in European circles, was appointed in after years to the governorship of the Vilayet of Broussa. During his residence in Europe he had collected a fine library, which he rightly considered the greatest ornament of his *konak*. But these reputed " infidel " writings gave umbrage to a fanatical old Dervish Sheikh of that city, who had great influence with the Pasha, and he resolved upon their destruction. With persuasive eloquence and prophetic promises, he so worked upon the mind of the Governor-General, that this dignitary was finally prevailed upon to consent to the destruction of his literary treasures, and, like those of Don Quixote, they were committed to the flames. The promised reward of this sacrifice was the much-desired and long-coveted post of Grand Vizier. Strange to say, the Pasha was actually called upon to occupy that high office, though he retained it only for the brief period of three days.

From the earliest times to the present, the most general, though at the same time the most harmless, weapon used against the Dervishes has been that of ridicule. Turkish and Persian literature teems

with satires,in proverb and story, on their peculiarities
of dress and practice. Even the mystic Sādi does
not spare them in his epigrams, though his satire
is chiefly directed against those who are Dervishes
in outward appearance only, as for instance :—

> Of what avail is frock or rosary,
> Or clouted garment ? Keep thyself but free
> From evil deeds, it will not need for thee
> To wear the " Crown " of felt, a Dervish be
> In heart, and wear the cap of Tartary.

A humorous story is current in the capital of a
Dervish whose ass, a present from his Sheikh, died
soon after he had set out on his pilgrimage. He
buried the animal by the roadside, and giving out
that a deceased companion was the occupant of
the newly-made grave, soon obtained from the
charitable passers-by sufficient funds to erect a
turbeh over it, of which he constituted himself the
guardian. Years passed. The *turbeh* became a
great place of pilgrimage ; miracles were performed
at it, and the fame of the rival shrine reached the
ears of the old Sheikh, who had heard no news of his
pupil since his departure, and lamented him as
dead. One day, accordingly, he locked up his
turbeh in order to pay a visit to his brother Sheikh.
He was hospitably received, and recognised the
rival *turbedji* as his former disciple.   When evening
came, and the last of the pilgrims visiting the shrine
had departed, the old Sheikh asked, with much
curiosity, *who* was the saint buried below, as he
knew of none formerly residing in that part of the
country. After some hesitation, Sheikh Ali confessed

that his dead ass was the only occupant of the tomb. As his superior did not seem much disturbed by the announcement, the younger Dervish ventured to enquire who was the Saint buried under his master's *turbeh*, and learnt at length that it was no other than the parent of his own sainted donkey !

The most wildly fanatical are found among the wandering Dervishes, who, by their prophecies and adjurations, often excite the Moslem population against their Christian neighbours. Shortly before the outbreak of the troubles in Bulgaria in 1876, one of these zealots completely terrorised the Christian inhabitants of Adrianople. He knocked at one door after another in the Christian quarter, forced his way in when they were opened, and declared to the startled inmates that Allah had revealed to Him his desire that the infidels of the town should be destroyed within three days after Easter. He finally reached the house of the Bishop, to whom he repeated his menacing prophecy. The reverend gentleman, apprehensive of the possible consequences to his flock of these " revelations," went at once to inform the Governor-General of the incident. The Dervish was sent for, asked if he had said what was reported of him, and what he meant by it. The wily ascetic, however, merely shrugged his shoulders and replied carelessly that, as he was in his *Hāl* when he made the alleged declaration, he was not responsible for anything he might have said. The Governor-General deemed it prudent to send him out of the city under escort

with orders for his conveyance to Broussa ; but
the Dervish managed to elude the vigilance of his
guards—possibly with their connivance—and continued his fanatical mission in other parts of the
province.

WORKS REFERRED TO IN THE
FOREGOING PAGES

ALI AZIZ EFFENDI, of Crete. *The Story of Jewād*, translated by
  E. J. W. GIBB, 16
BROWN, J. B.   *The Dervishes*, 18, 37, 149, 187
BROWNE, E. G.   *A Year Among the Persians*, 57-59
CLERMONT-GANNEAU.   *Revué Archeologique*, 22n.
CREASY, SIR E. S.   *History of the Ottoman Turks*, 19
CUNNINGHAM-GRAHAM, MRS.   *Life of St. Theresa*, 69n.
D'OHSSON.   *Tableau Générale de la Turquie*, 2n., 187
DOZY.   *Essai sur l'Islamisme*, 5n., 14
EVLIYA EFFENDI, *Narrative of Travels* (Oriental Translation
  Fund), 28, 33, 39, 40, 72, 166, 187
FALCONER, PROF.   The *Mesnevi*, translation of, 55
GARCIN DE TASSY.   *Mantic Uttair*, translation of the, 5n., 49
GASTON PARIS.   *Acad. des Inscriptions*, 22n
GIBB, E. J. W.   *Ottoman Poems*, 61-3, 119n.
GRIFFITH.   Translation of Jāmī's *Yusuf and Zulaikha*, 56n., 59,
  60
GUYARD.   *Revué de l'Histoire des Religions*, 22n.
JĀMĪ.   *Yusuf and Zulaikha : Salaman and Absal*, 1, 56-60
JELĀLŪ-'D-DĪN.   The *Mesnevi* or *Masnavi*, 50-55 ; 110
JONES, SIR WM.   *The Works*, vol. i, p. 52
LANE.   *The Modern Egyptians*, 35
MALCOLM.   *History of Persia*, 15, 153-4
MICHELET.   *La Sorcière*, 163
REDHOUSE, SIR J.   *The Mesnevi ; The Acts of the Adepts*,
  translations of, 31n., 51n., 69, 91, 156, 158, 161, 174
RILEY, ATHELSTAN.   *Mount Athos*, 77n.
ROZENZWEIG.   *Yusuf und Zulaikha*, 56n.
SĀDĪ.   *The Gulistan*, 35n.
SALE.   *Al Koran*, 72, 136-8, 143, 158
SILVESTRE DE SACY.   *Journal des Savants*, 2n.
SPRENGER.   *Journal of the Asiatic Society*, 5n.
UBICINI.   *Lettres sur la Turquie*, 46, 180, 188
VAUGHAN.   *Hours with the Mystics*, 5n.

INDEX

THE END